T0184612

Unity Networking Fundamentals

Creating Multiplayer Games with Unity

Sloan Kelly
Khagendra Kumar

Apress®

Unity Networking Fundamentals: Creating Multiplayer Games with Unity

Sloan Kelly
Niagara Falls, ON, Canada

Khagendra Kumar
Katihar, Bihar, India

ISBN-13 (pbk): 978-1-4842-7357-9
https://doi.org/10.1007/978-1-4842-7358-6

ISBN-13 (electronic): 978-1-4842-7358-6

Managing Director, Apress Media LLC: Welmoed Spahr
Acquisitions Editor: Spandana Chatterjee
Development Editor: Laura Berendson
Coordinating Editor: Divya Modi

Cover designed by eStudioCalamar

Cover image designed by Pixabay

Distributed to the book trade worldwide by Springer Science+Business Media New York, 1 New York Plaza, Suite 4600, New York, NY 10004-1562, USA. Phone 1-800-SPRINGER, fax (201) 348-4505, e-mail orders-ny@springer-sbm.com, or visit www.springeronline.com. Apress Media, LLC is a California LLC and the sole member (owner) is Springer Science + Business Media Finance Inc (SSBM Finance Inc). SSBM Finance Inc is a **Delaware** corporation.

For information on translations, please e-mail booktranslations@springernature.com; for reprint, paperback, or audio rights, please e-mail bookpermissions@springernature.com.

Apress titles may be purchased in bulk for academic, corporate, or promotional use. eBook versions and licenses are also available for most titles. For more information, reference our Print and eBook Bulk Sales web page at http://www.apress.com/bulk-sales.

Any source code or other supplementary material referenced by the author in this book is available to readers on GitHub via the book's product page, located at www.apress.com/978-1-4842-7357-9. For more detailed information, please visit http://www.apress.com/source-code.

Printed on acid-free paper

Table of Contents

About the Authors

Sloan Kelly has worked in the games industry for more than 13 years. He worked on a number of AAA and indie titles and currently works for an educational game company. He lives in Ontario, Canada with his wife and children. Sloan is on Twitter @codehoose and makes YouTube videos in his spare time.

Khagendra Kumar has worked with a number of educational institutions and game studios for training and solutions. He lives in Bihar, India and spends most of his time working with game AI. He can be reached via LinkedIn at /itskhagendra and on Instagram @Khagendra_Developer.

About the Technical Reviewer

 **Simon Jackson** is a long-time software engineer and architect with many years of Unity game development experience, as well as an author of several Unity game development titles. He both loves to both create Unity projects as well as lend a hand to help educate others, whether it's via a blog, vlog, user group, or major speaking event.

His primary focus at the moment is with the XRTK (Mixed Reality Toolkit) project, which is aimed at building a cross-platform Mixed Reality framework to enable both VR and AR developers to build efficient solutions in Unity and then build/distribute them to as many platforms as possible.

Introduction

This book sets out to demystify network programming and open you and your games up to the wider world using the Unity Engine and the C# programming language. The .NET framework that C# sits on top of has several classes that make creating networked games a little easier.

Intended Audience

This book is intended for Unity developers who are familiar with C# and want to implement their own networking framework, or those who want to have a better understanding of low-level network programming.

This is meant to be an introductory guide to networking. The book concentrates mostly on developing smaller games that can be run on your local network rather than larger multiplayer games played over the Internet. These basic concepts will help you better understand the underlying technology behind multiplayer games and the inherent constraints involved in passing data across a network. The last chapter of the book covers making your game available on the Internet using a third-party service.

Software and Hardware Requirements

The examples in this book were written using Unity 2020.1.6f1. I used both a MacBook Pro (mid-2012, Intel i7) and a PC (mid-2015, Intel i5) during the writing of this book and the examples. To run Unity, you will need a device that meets the following requirements:

- *Windows*: Windows 7 (SP1+)/Windows 10, 64-bit only, X64 architecture CPU with SSE2 instruction set support, DX10-, DX11-, or DX12-compatible GPU.

- *MacOS*: High Sierra 10.13+, X64 architecture CPU with SSE2 instruction set support, Metal-capable Intel or AMD GPU.

- *Linux (preview support)*: Ubuntu 16.04, 18.04, or CentOS 7, X64 architecture CPU with SSE2 instruction set support, OpenGL 3.2+ or Vulkan-compatible NVIDIA and AMD GPU, GNOME desktop environment. Requires proprietary NVIDIA or AMD graphics driver.

Be sure to check the Unity system requirements page for the most up-to-date information.

How This Book Is Organized

The book is organized into the following chapters:

- Networking basics

- Serialization

- UnityWebRequest and RESTful APIs

- Connected services with TCP

- Connectionless services with UDP

- Common networking issues

- First person maze shooter

- Remote connections

Source Code

The source code for this book is available on GitHub via the book's product page, located at www.apress.com/978-1-4842-7357-9. The source code contains everything you need to build the following:

- Real-time weather app

- Networked tic-tac-toe

- First person maze shooter

- Basic TCP and UDP examples

Conventions Used In This Book

Various typefaces and styles are used in this book to identify code blocks, warnings, and other notices.

C# code is written in this style:

```
if (player.IsLoggedIn)
{
        print("Player is logged in");
        server.PlayerAttached(player.ID);
}
```

This book contains a list of some tools that come with your operating system to help you. These all run from the command line, also known as the terminal or DOS prompt depending, on your operating system. Command lines are written in the following style. The $ at the beginning of the line should not be typed:

```
$ ls -al
```

If an issue needs special attention, the following block is used:

Note This is a call out and will alert you to any information that is important.

CHAPTER 1

Networking Concepts

This chapter covers the very basics of networking and introduces some tools that are beneficial when you need to debug your application. This chapter includes a brief overview of the client-server model, discusses how we will build the games in this book, and covers networking fundamentals that will help you understand and debug your games when developing the networking components.

By the end of this chapter, you will be familiar with the devices used to connect your PC to the outside world, how Internet addressing works, and what the client-server model is.

If you have an email account, surf the web, use social media, or play online games, you have used networking components. The modern Internet runs on a suite of protocols based on Transportation Control Protocol/Internet Protocol (TCP/IP).

Internet browsers like Chrome and Firefox use HTTP and HTTPS (HyperText Transport Protocol and HyperText Transport Protocol Secure, respectively) to communicate with remote servers. As shown in Figure 1-1, an encyclopedia is just a click away!

© Sloan Kelly and Khagendra Kumar 2022
S. Kelly and K. Kumar, *Unity Networking Fundamentals*,
https://doi.org/10.1007/978-1-4842-7358-6_1

Figure 1-1. *A Firefox browser containing the wikipedia.org home page*

The Firefox (or Chrome, Safari, or Edge) browser is a *client* that requests a document from a *server*. The server sends data back to the client. The client takes that data and renders it to the window. This is called the *client-server model*.

Client-Server Model

The client-server model is a distributed application structure. The responsibilities are divided between the client and the server. The client typically makes requests to the server and then displays the fetched information for the user. The server takes the request and processes it, returning the data back to the client. The server itself rarely displays any output.

Typically, the client and server run on two separate machines and are linked using a computer network. However, it is entirely possible for the client and the server to run on the same machine.

The client-server model allows multiple clients to access a single resource. For example, printers, documents on a hard drive, and remote compute power.

The client and the server need to speak the same language. In the case of a web client/server, this is HTTP/HTTPS, depending on the security of the site. To retrieve a document, users type an address into the address bar of the browser:

```
https://www.wikipedia.org
```

The `https://` indicates the protocol that will be used when communicating with the server. The part after the double slashes is the address of the server. The web client – the browser – will then make a request to the remote server using the HTTP language.

The request part of the message uses a verb like GET or POST and a resource name. For example:

```
GET /index.html HTTP/1.1
```

This statement says "Fetch me the `index.html` page using the HTTP version 1.1. protocol." The server will interpret this message and return the document to the client, as shown in Figure 1-2.

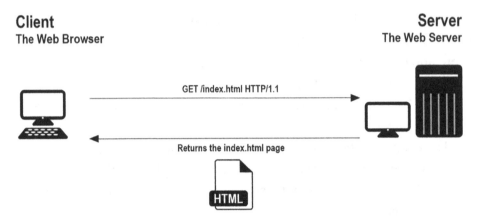

Figure 1-2. *The sequence of events fetching a document from a web server*

The web is one example of a client-server model.

The examples in this book show you how to create your own client-server model based games and how to write your own protocols to allow them to communicate effectively. In games, each player connects using a client to a remote server that contains all the rules for the game. Clients send movement information to the game server and the server updates the clients with new position and state data.

Connected vs. Connectionless Services

When you send a message across the Internet, it is split into many smaller messages called *packets*. These packets are routed all over the network and arrive at the destination. Some packets can take longer to arrive; some packets never make it. This is not good if you want your web page to arrive in one piece. Luckily, the web is a connection-oriented service and it guarantees that your message will arrive. Let's take a deeper look at connection- and connectionless-oriented services.

Packets

Your message is split into small packets and routed through the network. This is done for several reasons. It could be because a route to the server is blocked or because it is more efficient to group the packets and send them later when reaching a node in the network.

Your packets can arrive at the destination out of order, as shown in Figure 1-3.

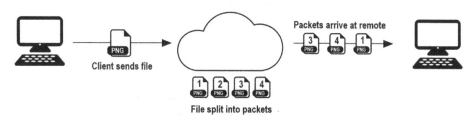

Figure 1-3. *File split into smaller packets, packet loss and packets received out of sequence*

In the example in Figure 1-3, the file is sent across the network in smaller packets numbered 1, 2, 3, and 4. As they travel through the network, Packet 2 is lost and Packet 4 arrives before Packet 3.

Sometimes packet loss is acceptable and other times it is not. It is up to the application developer to decide if packet loss or packets received out of sequence are acceptable side-effects. The developer will choose either a connection-oriented or connectionless-oriented approach, depending on the needs of the game. In a fast-moving game, some packet loss might be acceptable for the sake of maintaining speed.

Connection-Oriented Service

If you need to guarantee that messages arrive at the remote device in the correct order with no parts missing, you need to write a connection-oriented service.

Anything that uses Transport Control Protocol (TCP) will guarantee that packets arrive in order and the message you send will be intact. An example of an application that uses TCP is the web. HTTP is built using TCP to guarantee that messages arrive intact.

Using TCP, your client must establish a connection with a server to allow communication to flow between them. The connection can last any amount of time, from a couple of seconds to days. The connection is required to ensure that data is sent and received.

TCP provides error-free data transmission. If packets are dropped or corrupted, they are retransmitted. When packets arrive at their destination, the sender is notified.

Note   The error-free data transmission process is handled by the TCP protocol. Your code does not have to retransmit dropped packets. This is all handled for you by TCP on your machine's operating system.

As an example, the client in Figure 1-4 is transferring a PNG file to a remote server. A packet is dropped and the receiver sends a message back to the sender asking it to resend Packet 2. The sender obliges and resends Packet 2.

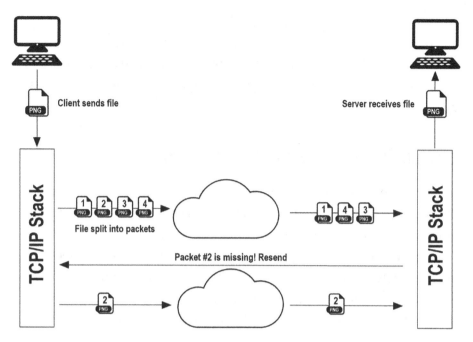

Figure 1-4. *Sequence showing the recovery of a dropped packet using TCP*

If your application needs to guarantee that transmitted messages appear in the correct order and are complete, use a TCP connection. Other applications for TCP include:

- Chat applications

- File transfer

- Mail services

The TCP/IP suite of applications is an example of a connection-oriented service. Example services are:

- POP/IMAP/SMTP for mail transfer

- FTP for file transfer

- HTTP for delivering web pages

The downside is that TCP is slower, due to the handshaking and confirmation messages that pass between the client and the server. If you do not care about the order of packets or don't care if any packets are dropped along the way, you can use a faster connectionless-oriented service.

Connectionless-Oriented Service

There are times when you do not need to guarantee delivery of packets. If they can arrive out of order, or not at all, you should consider creating a connectionless-oriented service.

In a connectionless-oriented service, the client does not connect with a server, it just sends the information. If the server cannot receive the packet, then it's lost. Because there is no connection, the number of messages sent per packet transferred is always just one – the packet being transferred.

Connectionless-oriented services are used for things like:

- Video streaming

- Multiplayer games

A video stream sends a minimum of 24 frames per second. It must get there very quickly ($1/24^{th}$ of a second) and so if one frame is lost there is not enough time to ask for another.

In multiplayer games, it is often too much overhead to use a TCP connection for game play. If the player input is sent at 60 frames per second (fps), then the occasional dropped packet will not make much difference. As you will see later in the book, there are ways around this.

The IP part of the TCP/IP offers a connectionless-oriented protocol called User Datagram Protocol (UDP). UDP allows developers to send so-called "fire and forget" messages to remote machines. There is no guarantee that the packets will arrive on time, or in sequence. If that is a sacrifice you're willing to make for speed, then UDP is a perfect choice.

Physical Network Devices

Devices like your mobile phone, PC, and tablet need to connect to a network. They do this using a *network card*. The formal name of this is a *network interface card* (NIC). Your device will connect to a local device called a *router* using either a WiFi (wireless) or an Ethernet (wired) connection.

Your router might be part of a cable or ADSL modem or a separate device altogether. The modem – short for modulator/demodulator – is a device that turns the received zeros and ones into wavelengths that can be passed down a wire and onto the Internet. Figure 1-5 shows a typical network diagram for a home network and a connection to a remote server like www.google.com.

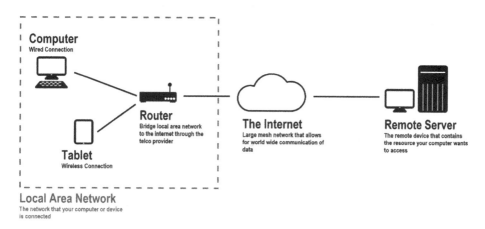

Figure 1-5. *Devices on your Local Area Network (LAN) connect through a router to the Internet*

All the traffic from your local devices to a remote server travels through the router. The router also provides another function that provides each connected device with a unique address on the LAN. This function is called *Dynamic Host Control Protocol*. This address will be used by other machines to communicate with each other.

There are two Internet Protocol address formats: IPv4 and IPv6. Each device will have an IPv4 and IPv6 address. This book uses IPv4 addresses. We cover addressing in the next section.

IPv4 and IPv6 are *logical addresses*. Each network card is assigned a *physical address* at the factory. This address is called the Media Access Control (MAC) address.

The architects of the original Internet — called DARPANet, short for Defense Advanced Research Projects Agency Network — used a mesh network, as shown in Figure 1-6.

LANs are connected to the Wider Area Network (WAN) or to the Internet using routers. The routers pass messages between each other until the destination is reached. This is why they are called *routers*; they route messages between nodes on the network. A *node* is a device connected to the network and can be a router or computer or any other network-accessible device.

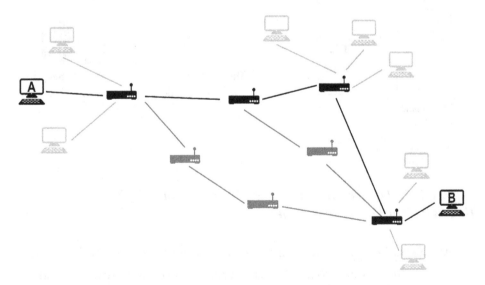

Figure 1-6. *Mesh network routing past disabled routers from Device A to B*

The mesh network allows the messages to be routed past broken or inaccessible parts of the network. When Device A wants to send a message to Device B, the devices on the network will reroute messages past the inactive nodes. Later, you will learn about a command-line tool that shows how messages are routed to a remote server.

The mesh network is an example of a network *topology*. Topology is just a fancy way of saying the shape of something. There are other network topologies:

- Bus – Each node on the network is connected to a single cable and T-connectors are used to connect PCs and other devices to the network.

- Ring – Data travels around the ring in one direction. Each device acts as a repeater to keep the signal strong. Every node is a critical link in the network.

- Star – This is the most common setup and the one that you have in your home. It's a central device, usually a router, connected to a larger network (your Internet Service Provider). Each local device connects to the router and thus out to the larger network.

- Tree – The tree topology is a combination of the star and bus.

Network Addressing

When you enter an address in the address box at the top of your browser and press Return, the page you requested appears after a few seconds. But how does the browser know where to go? This section explores the addresses used on the network, specifically with respect to the Internet.

So far, we have talked at a high level about data passing through a network using connection and connectionless services. How are these connected devices identified on the network? This section looks at how the IPv4 address system works and discusses the "uniqueness" of the number.

To connect to a network using TCP/IP, a device needs a network card of some kind. It can be wired or wireless. Each network card is given a "unique" hardware ID number called a MAC address. A network card is an electronic device that connects devices like computers, mobile phones, and games consoles to a computer network.

Media Access Control (MAC) Address

The MAC address is a group of six hexadecimal digits, like 01-23-45-67-89-ab. For example, the MAC address of the network card on my PC is C8-60-00-D0-5E-A5. MAC addresses are burned into the card and cannot be altered. This is the *physical address* of your device. The physical address is what identifies the device on the network.

The first three-digits of the MAC address identify the manufacturer. C8-60-00 is *ASUSTek Computer Inc.* That is the manufacturer of my computer's motherboard.

Because there are only six hexadecimal digits left, it would be impossible for manufacturers to give each device a unique physical ID. Instead, what they do is ship batches of network cards to different parts of the world to minimize the chances of two devices in the same location having the same address.

IP Address

The IP protocol uses a *logical address* to access devices on the network. This logical address is known as the IP address of the device. There are two ways to assign an IP address to a device; static and dynamic.

Static IP Addresses

The IP address can be set on the machine. This is a static address. This is usually only done for servers because these devices are known as endpoints in the network.

Dynamic IP Addresses

Dynamic IP addresses are assigned to each device when they boot up. The TCP/IP stack reaches out to the network to find a DHCP (Dynamic Host Control Protocol) server. The DHCP server assigns an address to the client. The dynamic addresses have a lease time, which means they expire and need to be renewed.

On my LAN, my PC seems to be given the same IP address, but it might not be the same on the network where your machine is connected.

IP Address Format

This book concentrates on IPv4 rather than IPv6. There are minor changes to the code to get it to run for IPv6, a flag or two to set.

The IPv6 address is much longer than its v4 counterpart. It consists of eight groups of four hexadecimal digits. An example IPv6 address is as follows:

```
1234:5678:9abc:def0:1234:5678:9abc:def0
```

On the contrary, IPv4 uses only four bytes separated by a period (.), such as:

```
192.168.1.1
```

Each digit in the IPv4 address is called an *octet* because it contains eight bits (one byte). The address's format is called *dotted decimal* because it contains four decimals separated by full stops. Four bytes is the same amount of space as an integer. This means that an IPv4 address can access up to 2^32 or 4.3 billion devices. But wait – aren't there more devices in existence than that? What about all the IoT (Internet of Things) devices like light bulbs, toasters, fridges, and the like?

It turns out that IPv4 was not enough and that is why we moved to IPv6. IPv4 gets around its limited address space by using *network segmentation*.

Note   For the remainder of this book, when referring to an IP address, it means an IPv4 address unless otherwise stated.

Address Classification

If you look at your machine's IP address using the `ipconfig` or `ifconfig` command (depending on your operating system), it is probably going to be something like 192.168.1.17 and your router is probably going to be located at address 192.168.1.1. A magic trick? No – most routers default to the Class C network, which is 192.168.1.x.

The IP addresses are split into several ranges. Each range represents the number of networks and the number of hosts that each network can contain. A host is just another name for a device. These ranges are called *classes*. There are also special IP addresses that you cannot use for your machine.

There are five classes of networks in the available IPv4 address ranges, called Classes A through E. Classes A to C are the ones most used because D and E are reserved classes. Table 1-1 shows each classification and describes what it means with respect to the available networks in that class and the number of hosts allowed per network.

Table 1-1. *Network Classes*

Class	Address Range	Supports
Class A	1.0.0.1 to 126.255.255.254	127 networks, 16 million hosts
Class B	128.1.0.1 to 191.255.255.254	16,000 networks, 65,000 hosts
Class C	192.0.1.1 to 223.255.254.254	2 million networks, 254 hosts
Class D	224.0.0.0 to 239.255.255.255	Reserved for multicast groups
Class E	240.0.0.0 to 254.255.255.254	Reserved for future use or experimental use only

Each network classification uses a *subnetwork mask*. This is a bitwise mask that you will be able to immediately tell the classification of your network. If you use the `ipconfig` command in Windows or `ifconfig` in Linux/Mac, you will see output similar to the this:

```
IPv4 Address. . . . . . . . . . . : 192.168.1.149
Subnet Mask . . . . . . . . . . . : 255.255.255.0
Default Gateway . . . . . . . . . : 192.168.1.1
```

More on this command later. There are two indications that the IPv4 address is a Class C address. The first is that the first octal is 192. The second is that the subnetwork mask is 255.255.255.0. This number is bitwise ANDed with the IP address on the local network to obtain the network, which would be 192.168.1.0..255 in this case.

There are special addresses that you cannot assign to your machine and have special meaning.

- The first is the *loopback address*. This is 127.0.0.1. That address is the machine you are using. If you start a service using that IP, it cannot be accessed from outside your computer.

15

- The second is the *broadcast address*. You can send a UDP message out onto the local area network using the address 255.255.255.255. This message will be sent to every device.

Note   IP addresses are unique to the local area network. However, they are not globally unique.

Domain Name System

When you type in the address for the Wikipedia website, you use text rather than an IP address. How does the web browser know how to translate the wikipedia.org text into an IP address? It uses a service called the *Domain Name System* (DNS).

The DNS is a fundamental part of the Internet. It matches up the name of the website's IP address. A website is just the server part of the web's client-server model. Each device that's connected to the network needs an address. The IP address for the website is the IP address for the server.

Most ISPs (Internet Service Providers – usually your telephone company) have their own DNS server. It is often best to use this server, because it will resolve addresses quicker.

A DNS server is simply a giant lookup table containing names of servers and their IP addresses. Listing 1-1 shows how this can be achieved using .NET's Dns.GetHostAddresses() function. It returns an array of IP addresses that can be used to access the server. The script will print the addresses to the console. You simply add the script to a GameObject in the scene of a Unity project and run the game.

Listing 1-1. Using Dns.GetHostAddresses() to Fetch the Addresses of the Google Server from the Current DNS

```
using System.Net;
using UnityEngine;

public class DnsLookup : MonoBehaviour
{
    public string url = "www.google.com";

    void Start()
    {
        System.Net.IPAddress[] addresses =
        Dns.GetHostAddresses(url);
        foreach (var address in addresses)
        {
            print(address);
        }
    }
}
```

When the game runs, you should see something like the following output in the console:

```
172.217.1.164
UnityEngine.MonoBehaviour:print (object)
DnsLookup:Start () (at Assets/Scripts/DnsLookup.cs:13)
```

Sockets and Ports

You will often hear people talking about network programming as *socket programming*. This is because network sockets are used in the TCP/IP suite. The combination of a port number and an IP address is called a *socket address*. You now know what an IP address is, so let's look at what a port number so that you can fully understand what a socket does.

What Is a Port Number?

When you connect to a remote machine, you need two things—the IP address of the remote machine and the port number that the service is running. Port numbers are in the range 1-65535, but you cannot use numbers below 256 because they are reserved for Internet services like FTP (21) and HTTP (80). Numbers in the range 256-1023 are also reserved for other well-known services. Anything from 1024 and above is available.

When you go to a website, your browser automatically tries to connect to port 80. You can force the browser to try another port by using a colon followed by the port number. For example, `http://127.0.0.1:8080` will try to access a web server running on port 8080.

By using different port numbers for each service, the computer can route calls to multiple services running on the same computer. For example, you can run a web server on port 80 and an FTP server on port 21, on the same computer. An FTP client will attach to the service running on 21, while a web client will ask the service running on port 80 for the wanted resource.

Games that host other players will have to expose themselves on a port number just like any other networked service.

What Is a Socket?

Not to be confused with a socket address, the singular socket class is a .NET representation of the Berkeley Socket. Let's take a trip down memory lane for this one. BSD is a flavor of the UNIX operating system and version 4.2 shipped with a programming interface that made network programming a lot easier. It was called *Berkeley Sockets*.

How did it make networking programming easier? In UNIX, everything is a file. When you open a file, a console, an input device like a keyboard, you get a file descriptor. This is a unique integer number representing the file you just opened. If you want to write to the file, you pass that number to the `write()` function.

When designing Berkeley Sockets, they chose to use this paradigm for their network programming interface. The socket() function returns a number that represents a file descriptor to a socket address. This number allows you to read and write to that socket address like you would a file. The socket address represents a connection to a remote machine.

The .NET framework has its own version of the low-level file descriptor, the *socket class*. This too references a socket address; an IP address plus port number.

Note   A socket file descriptor allows you to access a *socket address*, which is a combination of an IP address and a port number.

The socket class is low-level and for some situations it is useful. If you are using a connection-based service with TCP, though, there is a much better way in .NET, using network streams.

Open Systems Interconnection (OSI) Model

The TCP/IP suite is synonymous with the Internet. The suite dovetails quite nicely into the conceptual stack of protocols, known as the OSI seven-layer model, that allows communication between remote devices. These devices can be your computer, a mobile phone, a tablet, etc. The model itself does not describe how these devices talk to each other. Instead it focuses on the purpose of each layer.

The OSI model was created by the International Organization for Standardization (ISO) because during the early days of the Internet it was common for a large network of computers to use a variety of protocols. This led to network fragmentation. To clarify how a network should be set up, the OSI model was created, as shown in Figure 1-7.

Application	**End User Layer** The level seen by the user; the user interface	Your application and known services like POP, DNS, HTTP, FTP, SNMP, SMTP, SSH, etc.
Presentation	**Syntax Layer** Compression, standard formats and conversion	
Session	**Session Management** Authentication, permissions and session restoration	
Transport	**Host to Host** End-to-end error control	TCP, UDP
Network	**Packets** Network addressing, routing	IP, ICMP, ARP, DHCP
Data Link	**Frames** Error detection and flow control	Ethernet, PPP etc.
Physical	**Physical Structure** Cables, hubs etc. Physical medium, bits & voltages	

Figure 1-7. *The OSI seven-layer OSI model*

The model defines the Physical layer (the connections, voltages, etc.) to the Application layer. Reading from bottom to the top, each layer builds on the previous one and abstracts itself more and more. By the time you get to the top, where you will be building your games, you don't need to know about how data is routed through the network, or how error detection at the Data Link layer is handled. But it is nice to have a background in this process.

On the right side of Figure 1-7 are groups of protocols or services that use the accompanying layers. For example, the IP protocol sits at the Network layer. TCP and UDP sit at the Transport layer. Examples of services like POP (Post Office Protocol), DNS (Dynamic Name Service), and HTTP (HyperText Transport Protocol) use the Application, Presentation, and Session layers.

Now that we have explored some of the concepts, let's take a look at some command-line tools that will help you when you run into problems creating your networked games.

Command-Line Tools

There are several command-line tools that you should familiarize yourself with when creating a networked game, or indeed any application that uses networking. The examples in this section were run using Windows 10, but you can use the same commands on other operating systems too. There are notes for changes to make when using Ubuntu/macOS.

Commands are entered using the DOS prompt in Windows, or using the Terminal application in either Mac or Linux.

Opening a Command Prompt

To open a command prompt in Windows or terminal in Mac and Linux, follow the instructions for your operating system:

- Windows – Press the Window Key+R, type cmd, and press Return

- Mac – Press Command+Space, type terminal, and press Return

- Ubuntu – Press Ctrl+Alt+T

Hostname

The first command will display the name of your PC. This is handy if you want to give this information to other people on your network. Type hostname at the command prompt. The output will be the name of your host, which in my case is Sloan-PC:

```
$ hostname
Sloan-PC
```

Ping

The ping command is used to determine if your machine can "see" another machine. It sends a small packet of data to the remote machine and the time taken to reach the destination. If you've played multiplayer games, you're probably familiar with the name ping. Run the command with the name of the remote machine. Use the -4 option in Windows/Linux to show only the IPv4 addresses:

```
$ ping -4 www.google.com
Pinging www.google.com [172.16.1.86] with 32 bytes of data:
Reply from 172.16.1.86: bytes=32 time=3ms TTL=128
Reply from 172.16.1.86: bytes=32 time=3ms TTL=128
Reply from 172.16.1.86: bytes=32 time=2ms TTL=128
Reply from 172.16.1.86: bytes=32 time=2ms TTL=128

Ping statistics for 172.16.1.86:
    Packets: Sent = 4, Received = 4, Lost = 0 (0% loss),
Approximate round trip times in milli-seconds:
    Minimum = 2ms, Maximum = 3ms, Average = 2ms
```

If you are having issues connecting to a remote server, you can check that your machine is connected to the network using ping with 127.0.0.1:

```
$ ping -4 127.0.0.1
Pinging 127.0.0.1 with 32 bytes of data:
Reply from 127.0.0.1: bytes=32 time<1ms TTL=128
Reply from 127.0.0.1: bytes=32 time<1ms TTL=128
```

When a remote server is unavailable, it may be powered off or the network cable may be disconnected; you will see output like this:

```
$ ping -4 172.16.1.86
Pinging 172.16.1.86 with 32 bytes of data:
Request timed out.
```

IP Configuration

To list the IP configuration for your machine, use the `ipconfig` command. It will display the IP address, subnetwork mask, and default gateway of your current network connection. For Ubuntu and macOS, use `ifconfig`:

```
$ ipconfig
Windows IP Configuration

Ethernet adapter Ethernet:

   Connection-specific DNS Suffix  . :
   Link-local IPv6 Address . . . . . : fe80::...:64dc%13
   IPv4 Address. . . . . . . . . . . : 172.18.1.149
   Subnet Mask . . . . . . . . . . . : 255.255.255.0
   Default Gateway . . . . . . . . . : 172.16.1.1
```

You can share the IPv4 address with others on your LAN to allow them to connect to your PC. You will see a programmatic way to get this information later.

Address Resolution Protocol Cache

The Address Resolution Protocol is used to discover the Link Layer address – the MAC address – associated with an IPv4 address. The `arp` command displays the entries in the ARP cache. These are IP addresses that have been resolved to a given MAC address. Each device has a physical address (the MAC address) and, when a device connects to the network, the DHCP server assigns it a logical address (the IP address). The ARP shows the link between the logical and physical addresses.

Enter the arp -a command at the prompt to list the contents of the cache:

```
$ arp -a
Interface: 192.168.1.149 --- 0xd
  Internet Address        Physical Address        Type
  172.16.1.1              2c-56-dc-55-c0-c8       dynamic
  172.16.1.19             f0-18-98-14-e4-90       dynamic
  172.16.1.31             20-c9-d0-c9-60-53       dynamic
  172.16.1.46             3c-2a-f4-01-bb-c6       dynamic
  172.16.1.59             00-90-a9-cf-8a-b4       dynamic
  172.16.1.86             24-0a-64-3a-86-c5       dynamic
  172.16.1.110            00-09-b0-47-b0-df       dynamic
  172.16.1.117            c0-41-f6-5b-cb-e5       dynamic
  172.16.1.164            60-6d-3c-23-0b-74       dynamic
  172.16.1.173            f0-f0-a4-2a-ed-f4       dynamic
  172.16.1.230            b0-72-bf-4a-8d-02       dynamic
  172.16.1.243            00-a0-96-e8-fc-54       dynamic
  172.16.1.250            a0-ce-c8-d3-c6-46       dynamic
  172.16.1.255            ff-ff-ff-ff-ff-ff       static
  224.0.0.2              01-00-5e-00-00-02        static
  224.0.0.22             01-00-5e-00-00-16        static
  224.0.0.251            01-00-5e-00-00-fb        static
  224.0.0.252            01-00-5e-00-00-fc        static
  239.0.0.250            01-00-5e-00-00-fa        static
  239.255.255.250        01-00-5e-7f-ff-fa        static
  255.255.255.255        ff-ff-ff-ff-ff-ff        static
```

This command is handy if you suspect that two or more computers might be sharing the same IPv4 address. The "dynamic" and "static" refer to how the IP address was assigned. If the address was set on the machine, it is static; if it was assigned an IP address by a DHCP server, it is dynamic.

Network Status

The netstat command displays the active TCP/IP connections. If you are having issues with your application while it is running, this application might help you determine if you have connections. It is sometimes used with the grep or findstr command to filter the results. grep is short for *get regular expression* and, like findstr (*find string*), it can be used to filter the output from a command to cut down on the information displayed. Run the command without any options:

```
$ netstat
Active Connections
  Proto  Local Address    Foreign Address        State
  TCP    127.0.0.1:5354 Sloan-PC:61997         ESTABLISHED
  TCP    127.0.0.1:5354 Sloan-PC:61998         ESTABLISHED
  TCP    127.0.0.1:2701 Sloan-PC:56361         ESTABLISHED
  TCP    127.0.0.1:2701 Sloan-PC:61994         ESTABLISHED
  TCP    127.0.0.1:4966 Sloan-PC:49670         ESTABLISHED
  TCP    127.0.0.1:4967 Sloan-PC:49669         ESTABLISHED
  TCP    127.0.0.1:4969 Sloan-PC:49693         ESTABLISHED
  TCP    127.0.0.1:4969 Sloan-PC:49692         ESTABLISHED
  TCP    127.0.0.1:4993 Sloan-PC:49935         ESTABLISHED
  TCP    127.0.0.1:4993 Sloan-PC:49934         ESTABLISHED
```

The columns, from left to right, show the protocol used, the local address as a socket address (the IP and port number), the foreign (remote) address, which is also a socket address but, as shown here, can show names as well as IP addresses. The last column shows the state of the connection.

This will take some time to complete; it is usually a very long list. If you are using Windows, you can filter these results using the findstr command. For Ubuntu and macOS, use the grep command instead. To find all the HTTP connections, run the following:

```
$ netstat | grep ":http"
TCP 192.168.1.149:4969 server-13-249-130-224:http  CLOSE_WAIT
TCP 192.168.1.149:4999 ec2-99-80-242-242:https      CLOSE_WAIT
TCP 192.168.1.149:4999 ec2-99-80-242-242:https      CLOSE_WAIT
TCP 192.168.1.149:5004 ec2-99-80-242-242:https      CLOSE_WAIT
TCP 192.168.1.149:5005 ec2-99-80-242-242:https      CLOSE_WAIT
TCP 192.168.1.149:6406 yyz10s03-in-f5:https         TIME_WAIT
TCP 192.168.1.149:6407 52.114.74.43:https           ESTABLISHED
TCP 192.168.1.149:6408 220:https                    TIME_WAIT
```

The right-most column shows the status of the connection. In this example:

- CLOSE_WAIT – Means the connection is waiting for a connection termination request from the local user.

- TIME_WAIT – Means the connection is waiting for enough time to pass to be sure the remote TCP received the acknowledgement of its connection termination request.

- ESTABLISHED – Means the connection is open and the data was received and can be delivered to the user. This is the normal state for the data transfer phase of the connection.

If you are running Windows, the same output can be achieved using findstr:

```
$ netstat | findstr ":http"
```

Tracing the Route to the Server

To find the route that your messages take when transferring data to the remote machine, you can use the tracert command, which is traceroute on Mac and Linux. It takes a single parameter, which is the name of the host. For example, if I ping www.google.com:

```
$ tracert www.google.com
Tracing route to www.google.com [172.217.165.4]
over a maximum of 30 hops:
1   <1 ms   <1 ms   <1 ms   router.asus.com [172.16.1.1]
2    1 ms    1 ms    1 ms   192.168.0.1
3   10 ms   11 ms    7 ms   10.91.64.1
4   15 ms   12 ms   11 ms   10.0.75.209
5   19 ms   14 ms   11 ms   10.0.18.73
6   14 ms   15 ms   13 ms   209.85.173.40
7   14 ms   15 ms   13 ms   74.125.244.145
8   17 ms   13 ms   14 ms   216.239.40.255
9   14 ms   14 ms   11 ms   yyz12s06-in-f4.1e100.net
[172.217.165.4]
```

This shows the journey through the mesh network that the packet took. Remember that mesh networks are robust and the devices on the network will route packets a different way if nodes are not available. If you run this command multiple times, you might get multiple different routes.

From left to right, the columns are:

- The hop number, which represents the next node in the route. The first node is the local network's router. The last node (number 9) is the destination.

- At each hop, the `tracert` command makes three attempts to contact that node. These three numbers in milliseconds (ms) are the response times for each attempt.

- The last column is the IPv4 address of the node, or the name if it can be resolved.

Sometimes `tracert` can't determine the response time and you might see an asterisk (*) in one or more of the response time columns. This is usually okay and might just be an issue with the node. However, if your route does not get traced and you continually see a "Request Timed Out" message, there might be an issue with that node. It could be as simple as that particular node doesn't respond to pings.

Summary

There are many different parts to networking; this introductory chapter covered the basics that you need in order to understand how networking works "under the hood."

The Internet and by extension your local area network and your devices use the TCP/IP suite: Transport Control Protocol/Internet Protocol. This protocol is part of the OSI seven-layer conceptual networking model and describe how data is routed through the Internet.

There are two ways to send data across the network using the TCP/IP suite. One uses connection-based TCP and the other uses connectionless UDP.

We use IPv4 addressing in this text rather than the newer IPv6. IPv4 addresses are made up of four octals (bytes).

Every device has a physical address (MAC) and a logical address (IP). Each machine can be given a name that is exposed through the Domain Name System (DNS), allowing you to use words rather than IP addresses to find remote servers.

Services running on a host use another type of address, called a socket address, that contains both the IP address of the host and the port number. A socket is also a name given to a low-level object that can be used to send and receive data to and from the socket address.

There is a set of useful command-line tools available on all modern operating systems to help you debug your application if you run into problems.

CHAPTER 2

Serialization

Serialization is the process of taking data in memory and reformatting it to store, to send it across the network, or to construct an object in memory. A large part of message transmission and reception processes in networking use object serialization. This chapter covers the two serialization formats used in this book: JSON and binary.

Serialization Basics

In its basic form, serialization takes the public properties or fields of an instance of a class or struct and writes the name and value of them to disk or sends them across the network. The collection of property names and values is called the *state* of an object at a particular time. It is this state that you want to capture for storage or for transmission across the network.

Serialization is taking a snapshot of the current state of the class or struct instance. When an object is created, it automatically has the methods needed to manipulate its data. The state is the value that the player has given the object, either directly or indirectly during their interaction with the game.

Uses for serialization include:

- *Player data.* When the player returns to the game, their save state is restored and they can begin where they left off.

© Sloan Kelly and Khagendra Kumar 2022
S. Kelly and K. Kumar, *Unity Networking Fundamentals*,
https://doi.org/10.1007/978-1-4842-7358-6_2

- *Telemetry.* Usage data can be sent to analytic services to determine how many people have completed a particular level or how many people bought a particular item of clothing in the game.

- *Networking.* Sending data from one machine to another to update a player's position or to send a chat message.

JSON

JavaScript Object Notation (JSON), as you might get from the name, is derived from JavaScript and is language-independent. A number of languages have adopted its usage to serialize data. JSON has become the go-to data format for the web and is now ubiquitous. It is a collection of key-value pairs in a human-readable form. The *key* is the name of the field or property and the *value* is the data the field or property contains at the time the instance was serialized.

For example, in Listing 2-1, the JSON object describes a player object with character data.

Listing 2-1. JSON Data Containing Character Information

```
{
        "name": "El Player",
        "lives": 3,
        "completed_levels": [1, 2, 3, 4],
        "last_pos": {
                "x": 10,
                "y": 15
        }
}
```

The JSON file format has the following requirements:

- Property names must be wrapped in double quotation marks.

- A JSON object starts and ends with braces ({ and }).

- A string must be wrapped in double quotation marks.

- Numbers (integers and decimals) and Boolean values are typed as is, without quotes.

- Arrays start and end with square brackets ([and]).

- Elements are separated with commas (,).

Unity has a built-in utility class called `JsonUtility` that makes creating JSON formatted strings and reconstructing objects from those strings very easy. There are two main static methods in `JsonUtility`:

- `ToJson()` takes an object and creates the JSON-formatted string.

- `FromJson<T>()` takes the JSON-formatted string and converts it to an object of type `T`.

Let's look at this process in action by creating a Unity project.

Simple JSON Serialization/Deserialization

Follow these instructions to set up the project.

1. Create a new 2D project in Unity called `json-serialization-example`.

2. Create a folder called `Scripts` in the `Assets` folder.

3. Inside the Scripts folder, create two C# scripts:
    JsonSerializationExample and BasicObject.

4. Drag and drop the JsonSerializationExample
    script onto the main camera object in the scene.

Once you have the project set up, double-click the BasicObject script
file to open the C# file in Visual Studio (or your code editor of choice).
When the code editor opens, change the BasicObject.cs file to look like
Listing 2-2.

Listing 2-2. The BasicObject That Will Be Serialized and
Deserialized to and from JSON

```
using System;
using UnityEngine;

[Serializable]
public class BasicObject
{
    public Vector3 position;
    public string name;
    public int health;
    public int shield;
}
```

The class does not have a constructor. Having a constructor would
cause problems when an attempt is made to deserialize the object. The
deserializer would try to create an instance of the object but wouldn't be
able to find a non-parameterized constructor. You can get around this by
creating two constructors—one with parameters to set the initial state and
a parameterless constructor for serialization. Because it is a simple data
object, I have chosen to omit constructors completely.

Any class that's used to serialize data should have the Serializable attribute (located in the System namespace) applied to it.

Note   Attribute classes are used in C# to provide additional information at runtime about the class, class member, or parameter to which the class has been applied.

The class also contains the Vector3 Unity class. The JSON serializer will have no problem serializing this field because it is part of the Unity Engine. In general, though, class instances you want to serialize should extend from MonoBehaviour or ScriptableObject, or plain class or structs with the [Serializable] attribute.

Save the file and open the JsonSerializationExample script file. Change the JsonSerializationExample.cs file to match Listing 2-3.

Listing 2-3. The JsonSerializationExample Script that Will Serialize and Deserialize an Object to and from JSON

```
using UnityEngine;

public class JsonSerializationExample : MonoBehaviour
{
    void Start()
    {
        var basicObject = new BasicObject
        {
            shield = 100,
            health = 50,
            name = "Sven The Explorer",
            position = new Vector3(1, 2, 3)
        };
```

```
        string json = JsonUtility.ToJson(basicObject);
        Debug.Log(json);

        BasicObject copy = JsonUtility.
        FromJson<BasicObject>(json);
        Vector3 pos = copy.position;
        Debug.Log($"{copy.name} at {pos.x}, {pos.y}, {pos.z}");
    }
}
```

When the game runs, you should see the following output in the console.

```
{"position":{"x":1.0,"y":2.0,"z":3.0},"name":"Sven The Explorer",
"health":50,"shield":100}
UnityEngine.Debug:Log (object)
JsonSerializationExample:Start () (at Assets/Scripts/
JsonSerializationExample.cs:17)

Sven The Explorer at 1, 2, 3
UnityEngine.Debug:Log (object)
JsonSerializationExample:Start () (at Assets/Scripts/
JsonSerializationExample.cs:21)
```

In Listing 2-3, an instance of BasicObject is constructed. Because I opted not to create constructors, you can see that the initialization here is a similar format to the JSON in that it contains key-value pairs. The order doesn't matter at all. This instance is passed to the ToJson() static method of JsonUtility from the UnityEngine namespace and a string is returned. This is the JSON string-formatted version of the object. The JSON string is printed to the console window. The output is shown in Figure 2-1.

The JSON string is then passed into the static method FromJson<T>() of the JsonUtility and a new instance of BasicObject is created with the values from the original object applied to it. To fit on the line, I assigned the copy's position field to a temporary variable called pos. This keeps the code to one line in this book. You could have easily used `copy.position.x` and so on in the interpolated string that displays the values of the newly created object.

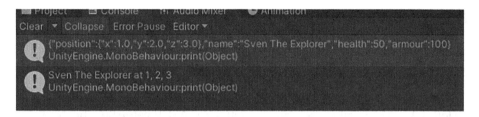

Figure 2-1. *The output of the two Debug.Log() functions in the JsonSerializationExample script*

As you can see, the JSON format is great for humans, because it's really easy to read. You can immediately see the property and field values – the state of the object and the file is structured in such a way that you can see the object's hierarchy.

When using the `UnityWebRequest` object to transfer data back and forth between a remote web server, you will use the JSON string as your medium. However, in order to transmit this data across the network using sockets, you need to perform an additional step. You need to convert the string into a series of bytes, because bytes (in the form of 0s and 1s) is how data transmission happens using sockets.

Even though JSON is a good store of the object's current state, it cannot be used to transmit across a network. All the methods used to send and receive data across the network use streams of bytes. In code this means that you need to convert the data you want to transmit to an array of bytes. Similarly on the receiving end of the communication, the bytes retrieved must be converted back.

Note   JSON is how you store a snapshot of an object's state; bytes is how you transfer that state across the network.

Binary Representation of a String

We are going to use the ASCII (American Standard Code for Information Interchange) text format to send and receive data. ASCII is a lookup table where an integer represents a shape displayed onscreen. For example, the letter A is ASCII value 65, while the letter Z is ASCII value 90. The .NET framework provides easy ways to encode and decode messages in this format. And it provides methods to convert a string to and from an array of bytes.

We are going to use the GetBytes() method to convert the string into a series of bytes and the GetString() method to convert the bytes to a string. GetBytes() is used during serialization. GetString() is used during deserialization. Both of these methods are in the Encoding.ASCII class. The changes to the script are in bold in Listing 2-4.

Listing 2-4. The Binary Version of the JSON Serializer. Additional Lines Shown in Bold

```
using System.Text;
using UnityEngine;

public class JsonSerializationExample : MonoBehaviour
{
    void Start()
    {
        var basicObject = new BasicObject
        {
            shield = 100,
            health = 50,
```

```
        name = "Sven The Explorer",
        position = new Vector3 { x = 1, y = 2, z = 3 }
    };

    string json = JsonUtility.ToJson(basicObject);
    Debug.log(json);

    byte[] bytes = Encoding.ASCII.GetBytes(json);
    Debug.Log($"{bytes[0]:x} {bytes[1]:x} {bytes[2]:x}
    {bytes[3]:x}");

    string jsonFromBytes = Encoding.ASCII.GetString(bytes);
    BasicObject copy = JsonUtility.FromJson<BasicObject>(js
    onFromBytes);
    Vector3 pos = copy.position;
    Debug.Log($"{copy.name} at {pos.x}, {pos.y}, {pos.z}");
    }
}
```

The output from the console window should look similar to this:

```
{"position":{"x":1.0,"y":2.0,"z":3.0},"name":"Sven The Explorer
","health":50,"shield":100}
UnityEngine.Debug:Log (object)
JsonSerializationExample:Start () (at Assets/Scripts/
JsonSerializationExample.cs:17)
7b 22 70 6f
UnityEngine.Debug:Log (object)
JsonSerializationExample:Start () (at Assets/Scripts/
JsonSerializationExample.cs:20)
Sven The Explorer at 1, 2, 3
UnityEngine.Debug:Log (object)
JsonSerializationExample:Start () (at Assets/Scripts/
JsonSerializationExample.cs:25)
```

The JSON string is converted to a byte array. This byte array is what you send across the network. In this example, though, the additional print statement displays the first four bytes of the array to show you its contents. I used the :x option to format the numbers in hexadecimal.

If you convert those numbers to ASCII values, as shown in Table 2-1, you can see that they represent the characters { "po, which are the first four characters of the JSON string.

Table 2-1. *The First Four Bytes of the Message with their ASCII Values Shown as Hexadecimal and Decimal Values*

Hexadecimal	Decimal	ASCII Character
7b	123	{
22	34	"
70	112	P
6f	111	0

Binary

The JSON format is verbose. It contains information about the data that you might not want or need to transmit. An alternative is to create a binary representation of your data. This can be achieved by using *structs* to hold the data and data marshaling to get the struct into a byte array.

Marshaling is the process of taking an object like a struct and transforming it into a format suitable for storage or transmission. That sounds a lot like serialization! In fact, marshaling is one form of serialization. Marshaling maintains the shape of the data so that when it's de-marshaled, the object can be constructed again. Marshaling in .NET is used to share data between the managed memory of .NET and the unmanaged memory owned by the program.

Managed memory allows for easy garbage collection within your C# program. Unmanaged memory can be accessed by Windows systems outside of the .NET environment. For example, if you want to make low-level system calls. The major difference between the two is how the memory is freed. When using unmanaged memory, it us up to the programmer to free the memory. Managed memory is freed when the program terminates.

Marshaling provides you with an easy way to convert an object to a byte array.

Simple Binary Serialization/Deserialization

Follow these instructions to set up the project.

1. Create a new 2D project in Unity called `binary-serialization-example`.

2. Create a folder called `Scripts` in the `Assets` folder.

3. Inside the `Scripts` folder, create two C# scripts: `BinarySerializationExample` and `MyData`.

4. Drag and drop the `BinarySerializationExample` onto the main camera object in the scene.

Once you have the project set up, double-click the `MyData` script file to open the C# file in Visual Studio (or your code editor of choice). When the code editor opens, change the `MyData.cs` file to look like Listing 2-5.

Listing 2-5. The MyData Structure

```
using System;
using System.Runtime.InteropServices;
using UnityEngine;
```

```csharp
[Serializable]
[StructLayout(LayoutKind.Sequential, Pack = 1)]
public struct MyData
{
    public Vector3 position;

    [MarshalAs(UnmanagedType.ByValTStr, SizeConst = 128)]
    public string name;
    public int health;
    public int shield;

    public override string ToString()
    {
        return $"{name}, health: {health}, shield: {shield}
        @ {position}";
    }
}
```

The contents of the struct are almost the same as the data from the JSON example. There are a couple of additional attributes, though: StructLayout and MarshalAs. These are part of the interoperation services (interop services) between .NET and COM (Common Object Model) used by Windows. To use these services, you must include the System.Runtime.InteropServices namespace.

The StructLayout attribute is required because .NET determines the most efficient way to pack data. You might assume that the data will be stored in the order that you write it in code, but that might not be the case. To force .NET to keep the order that you used, you must apply the StructLayout attribute with the LayoutKind.Sequential option. The Pack parameter specifies the padding value. By setting it to 1, you make sure that the struct is not padded and takes up the number of bytes specified, i.e., an integer takes four bytes.

The MarshalAs attribute is used on the string field *name* because the marshaler needs to know the size of the strings. Always specify the least amount of storage for this. If it is possible to compress the name into a smaller size, try to do that to minimize the overall size of the structure.

Save this file.

Listing 2-6 shows the contents of the .cs file. Open this file and change its contents to the following.

Listing 2-6. The BinarySerializationExample Class

```
using System.Runtime.InteropServices;
using UnityEngine;

public class BinarySerializationExample : MonoBehaviour
{
    void Start()
    {
        var data = new MyData
        {
            shield = 100,
            health = 50,
            name = "Sven The Destroyer",
            position = new Vector3(1, 2, 3)
        };

        Debug.Log($"Original: {data}");

        byte[] bytes = ToBytes(data);
        MyData copy = ToObject<MyData>(bytes);

        Debug.Log($"Copy: {copy}");
    }
```

```
/// <summary>
/// Deserialize an array of bytes and return an
/// instance of object type T with the serialized data.
/// </summary>
/// <typeparam name="T">Class or Struct type to be
    created</typeparam>
/// <param name="data">Array of bytes containing serialized
    data</param>
/// <returns>An instance of object type T</returns>
private T ToObject<T>(byte[] data)
{
    // Create an area of memory to store the byte array and
    // then copy it to memory
    var size = Marshal.SizeOf(typeof(T));
    var ptr = Marshal.AllocHGlobal(size);
    Marshal.Copy(data, 0, ptr, size);

    // Using the PtrToStructure method, copy the bytes out
    // into the Message structure
    var copyData = (T)Marshal.PtrToStructure(ptr, typeof(T));
    Marshal.FreeHGlobal(ptr);
    return copyData;
}

/// <summary>
/// Serialize an object to an array of bytes.
/// </summary>
/// <param name="data">The object to be serialized</param>
/// <returns>The serialized object as an array of bytes
    </returns>
private byte[] ToBytes(object data)
{
```

```
// Create a pointer in memory and allocate the size of
the structure
var size = Marshal.SizeOf(data);
byte[] buf = new byte[size];
var ptr = Marshal.AllocHGlobal(size);

// Copy the structure to the newly created memory space
// and then copy it to the byte buffer
Marshal.StructureToPtr(data, ptr, true);
Marshal.Copy(ptr, buf, 0, size);

// Always free your pointers!
Marshal.FreeHGlobal(ptr);
return buf;
    }
}
```

The Start() method creates an instance of the MyData structure and fills it with data. A copy of the data structure is created. The contents of the original instance and the copy are printed to the console when the game runs, as shown in Figure 2-2.

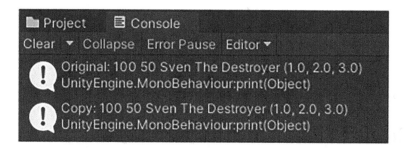

Figure 2-2. *The output from the binary serialization example*

The two methods of interest in this example are the ToBytes() and ToObject() methods.

Creating a Byte Array from a Struct

Creating a byte array from a struct involves copying the struct to unmanaged memory and copying the contents of that unmanaged memory back to managed memory in the array.

In order to allocate the right amount of memory, the object's size is required. In this case, it's the size of the MyData structure. The size of a structure is determined by the size of each of the elements. In this case:

- One Vector3 = 4 float values = 4 * 4 bytes = 16

- Two integers = 2 * 4 bytes = 8

- One string = 128

The total size of this struct is 152 bytes. To create a byte array from a struct, follow these steps as performed in the ToBytes() method:

1. Create a byte buffer (an array) to hold the resulting bytes.

2. Allocate memory from the unmanaged memory of the process that will hold the struct data.

3. Copy the structure to the unmanaged memory using the StructureToPtr() method.

4. Copy the data stored in the unmanaged memory to the byte array.

5. Free up the unmanaged memory.

Re-Create an Object from a Byte Array

Once you have the object in a byte array, the natural next step is to create a copy of the object at the other end. As might be expected, this is the opposite of the method required to place the object in a byte array.

To re-create the struct from a byte array, follow these steps as performed in the ToObject() method:

1. Allocate enough unmanaged memory to hold the structure.

2. Copy the byte array into the unmanaged memory.

3. Use the PtrToStructure() method to extract the structure from unmanaged memory.

4. Free up the unmanaged memory.

Note   Unmanaged memory is not freed by .NET when your program exits! To avoid memory leaks, always free up unmanaged memory!

The Network Library NetLib

To make things easier and so that you're not duplicating a lot of code, I'm going to suggest that you create a network library to store helper functions and classes that you will build on throughout the book.

I'm going to start by creating extension methods for marshaling/unmarshaling structs and for conversion between JSON to byte arrays and back again.

Use the same project as the binary serialization example. You can always make a Unity package for the NetLib, or just copy the folder to the new project later.

To create the NetLib folder, follow these steps:

1. In the Scripts folder, create a new folder called NetLib.

2. In the Scripts folder, create a new C# script file called BinarySerializationWithNetLib.

3. Open the NetLib folder.

4. Create two new C# script files inside the NetLib
    folder: JsonExtensions and StructExtensions.

5. Save the current scene.

6. Create a new scene called NetLibExample.

7. Drag the BinarySerializationWithNetLib script to
    the camera.

You should now have the folder structure shown in Figure 2-3.

Figure 2-3. *The folder structure of the binary project with the new
classes in the correct folders*

Once you have completed all these steps, double-click the
JsonExtensions file to open it and replace its contents with the ones
shown in Listing 2-7.

Listing 2-7. The JsonExtensions Class

```
using System.Text;
using UnityEngine;

public static class JsonExtensions
{
    public static byte[] ToJsonBinary<T>(this T data) where T:
    new()
    {
        string json = JsonUtility.ToJson(data);
        return Encoding.ASCII.GetBytes(json);
    }

    public static T FromJsonBinary<T>(this byte[] data) where
    T: new()
    {
        string json = Encoding.ASCII.GetString(data);
        return JsonUtility.FromJson<T>(json);
    }
}
```

These static methods use similar code that was created for the JsonSerializationExample script. ToJsonBinary() is an extension method for objects to help serialize them to a byte array containing JSON data. FromJsonBinary() is an extension method for byte arrays to convert the contents to an instance of an object. Save the file.

Open the StructExtensions script file and replace it with the code in Listing 2-8. These are the same methods, slightly renamed, that were used in the binary serialization example.

49

Listing 2-8. The StructExtensions Class

```
using System.Runtime.InteropServices;

public static class StructExtensions
{
    public static T ToStruct<T>(this byte[] data) where T: struct
    {
        var size = Marshal.SizeOf(typeof(T));
        var ptr = Marshal.AllocHGlobal(size);
        Marshal.Copy(data, 0, ptr, size);

        var copyData = (T)Marshal.PtrToStructure(ptr, typeof(T));
        Marshal.FreeHGlobal(ptr);
        return copyData;
    }

    public static byte[] ToArray (this object data)
    {
        var size = Marshal.SizeOf(data);
        byte[] buf = new byte[size];
        var ptr = Marshal.AllocHGlobal(size);

        Marshal.StructureToPtr(data, ptr, true);
        Marshal.Copy(ptr, buf, 0, size);

        Marshal.FreeHGlobal(ptr);
        return buf;
    }
}
```

Save the file.

Tying these classes together is the `BinarySerializationWithNetLib` class. Open this file and replace it with the code in Listing 2-9.

Listing 2-9. The Basic BinarySerializationWithNetLib Class

```
using UnityEngine;

public class BinarySerializationWithNetLib : MonoBehaviour
{
    void Start()
    {
    }
}
```

Each of the listings that follow will be added one at a time to the `Start()` method. Listing 2-10 creates the instance of the `MyData` class and assigns some values to the instance. A debug statement outputs the contents to the console.

Listing 2-10. Creating the MyData Instance

```
        MyData data = new MyData
        {
            shield = 100,
            health = 50,
            name = "Sven The Destroyer",
            position = new Vector3(1, 2, 3)
        };

        Debug.Log($"Original: {data }");
```

Because you're using extension methods, the code looks a lot cleaner and you don't need to place additional functions in each class that requires it. Static helper methods could be used, but extension methods are cleaner because they are attached to the object. This elegance can be seen in Listing 2-11, which shows how the structure is marshaled into a byte array using the `ToArray()` extension method and re-created using the `ToStruct()` extension method. To demonstrate that it worked, a debug print statement outputs the contents of the copy.

Listing 2-11. Performing a Binary Serialization/Deserialization

```
byte[] bytes = data.ToArray();
MyData copy = bytes.ToStruct<MyData>();

Debug.Log($"Copy: {copy}");
```

Last but not least, Listing 2-12 uses the extension methods
`ToJsonBinary()` and `FromJsonBinary()` to serialize/deserialize an object
to and from the binary JSON format. A debug print displays the contents of
the copy.

Listing 2-12. JSON Serialization/Deserialization Using Extension
Methods

```
byte[] jsonBytes = data.ToJsonBinary();
MyData jsonCopy = jsonBytes.FromJsonBinary<MyData>();
Debug.Log($"Json Copy: {jsonCopy}");
```

Save the file. When it runs, the program produces the output shown in
Figure 2-4.

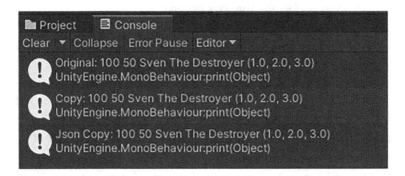

Figure 2-4. *The output showing the original, the binary copy, and
the JSON copy*

The complete listing of the `BinarySerializationWithNetLib` class is
shown in Listing 2-13.

Listing 2-13. The Completed BinarySerializationWithNetLib Class

```
using UnityEngine;

public class BinarySerializationWithNetLib : MonoBehaviour
{
    // Start is called before the first frame update
    void Start()
    {
        // Create an instance of the data to be serialized/
        deserialized
        var data = new MyData
        {
            shield = 100,
            health = 50,
            name = "Sven The Destroyer",
            position = new Vector3(1, 2, 3)
        };

        Debug.Log($"Original: {data}");

        // Make a copy of the data
        byte[] bytes = data.ToArray();
        MyData copy = bytes.ToStruct<MyData>();

        Debug.Log($"Copy: {copy}");

        // And now some JSON
        // Make a copy of the data and serialize it to JSON and
        // back again
        byte[] jsonBytes = data.ToJsonBinary();
        MyData jsonCopy = jsonBytes.FromJsonBinary<MyData>();
        Debug.Log($"Json Copy: {jsonCopy}");
    }
}
```

Summary

Serialization is the process of taking an in-memory object and storing the contents of its various fields, also known as the *object's state,* to disk or for transmission across the network. This book uses two types of serialization—JSON and binary. While JSON is a string-based format, you need to convert that string to a byte array for transmission across the network. JSON is how you store a snapshot of an object's state; bytes are how you transfer that state across the network.

Binary serialization involves using only structs. These structs are marshaled from managed memory into unmanaged memory as a sequence of bytes. Those byte sequences are read back into unmanaged memory. The .NET runtime will clean up managed memory used by the game when it terminates. However, it will not clean up unmanaged memory used by the program. It is the programmer's responsibility to free unmanaged memory consumed by the program. Memory allocated as part of this operation in the unmanaged space must be freed up to prevent memory leaks.

The next chapter provides an example of serialization/deserialization using a remote weather service. Data will be queried for using URLs and the returned message will be a JSON string.

CHAPTER 3

RESTful APIs

Up to this point, you have been learning about low-level concepts when it comes to networking. For the most part, though, network programming is done at the Application layer. This is the top-most layer of the OSI model, as shown in Figure 3-1, where your game sits.

Application	**End User Layer** The level seen by the user; the user interface	Your application and known services like POP, DNS, HTTP, FTP, SNMP, SMTP, SSH, etc.
Presentation	**Syntax Layer** Compression, standard formats and conversion	
Session	**Session Management** Authentication, permissions and session restoration	
Transport	**Host to Host** End-to-end error control	TCP, UDP
Network	**Packets** Network addressing, routing	IP, ICMP, ARP, DHCP
Data Link	**Frames** Error detection and flow control	Ethernet, PPP etc.
Physical	**Physical Structure** Cables, hubs etc. Physical medium, bits & voltages	

Figure 3-1. *The OSI seven-layer network model*

Your game might utilize some form of web service to get data for your game, such as leaderboards, friend's lists, etc.

© Sloan Kelly and Khagendra Kumar 2022
S. Kelly and K. Kumar, *Unity Networking Fundamentals*,
https://doi.org/10.1007/978-1-4842-7358-6_3

The `UnityWebRequest` class can be used to connect to a web server and perform web requests. It is possible to write your own code to do this using Sockets or TcpClient, but because this class exists and provides a lot of the functionality that you need already, it's best to use it instead. Among other features, it can be used to get data from web pages using what is known as RESTful APIs.

What Is a RESTful API?

In its simplest form, a RESTful API is a way for clients to request data using a web URL (Uniform Resource Locator) and the request can be given a response in a known format from the server. The client can use HTTP verbs like GET, PUT, and DELETE to perform actions on the data. This matches up with typical CRUD (Create, Read, Update and Delete) operations like getting leaderboard data, saving or replacing player state, and deleting a save slot, for example. This means that the client does not have to be written in the same language as the server. Because the requests use URLs and standard HTTP messages, there is no need to open additional ports. The developer just needs to be able to request a web page to read or write information.

REST is short for *REpresentational State Transfer*. API is short for *Application Programming Interface.* As long as the client and the server agree on the messages – the format of the requests and their responses – and how those requests are made using HTTP, both the client and the server will understand the messages passed between them.

Note   REST is a concept; it does not define the API. APIs are different for each service.

As shown in Figure 3-2, a request is made to a website using a RESTful call. The response that returns is a JSON string.

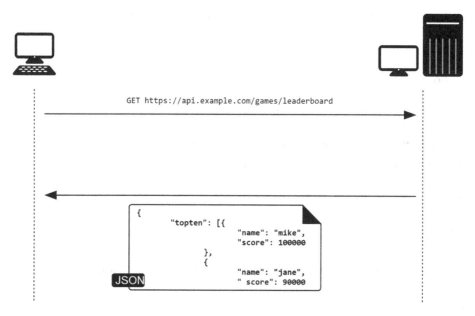

Figure 3-2. *A RESTful request and response showing a GET request for a leaderboard and the JSON response that's returned*

RESTful Requests

Each URL that's used to access a RESTful API is called a *request* and it is made up of four things:

- An endpoint

- A method

- Headers

- The data, also known as the body

The Endpoint

This is the URL that forms the request for the data you need. It is somewhat arbitrary and depends on the API creator, but it follows the structure:

```
https://server/path/feature/sub-feature
```

For example:

```
https://api.example.com/games/leaderboard
```

There is also a root endpoint. This is the starting point of the API and usually includes the protocol. For example:

```
https://api.example.com
```

A Method

The path is what comes after the root endpoint. For example:

```
/games/leaderboard
```

You need to look at the service's API documentation to see the paths that it offers. For example, there is extensive documentation for the Steam API at `https://developer.valvesoftware.com/wiki/Steam_Web_API`. You could think of paths as being synonymous with functions and methods in a normal program.

Sometimes a path in an API document will specify a colon. This means that you should put in a value there. For example, let's say your service has leaderboards for lots of games. You might see a path defined in a document as follows:

```
/games/:gamename/leaderboard
```

To access the leaderboard of your game called "Jump Game" for example, you might have a path like so:

```
/games/jump-game/leaderboard
```

The Headers

The headers provide extra information to the client and server. Headers can be used for a number of reasons, including authentication and providing additional metadata to the receiving device.

HTTP headers are property-value pairs that are separated by a colon. The following example shows a header that identifies the content as a JSON string:

```
Content-Type: application/json
```

The Data

The data is sometimes called the body or the message. It contains information that you want to send to the server. This option is only used with POST, PUT, PATCH, and DELETE requests. Examples are shown in Table 3-1.

Table 3-1. *HTTP Verbs and Their Uses*

HTTP Verb	Use
POST	Create something new on the server, such as when a player logs in for the first time.
PUT	Create or update. This could be used when saving player state to the server.
PATCH	Update a small amount of information. For example, when the player updates their password.
DELETE	Remove something from the game. For example, when a player deletes their account.

RESTful Responses

The format of the response varies from service to service but it is typically formatted as a JSON string. This string can be easily converted into a class using a JSON parser like the one provided by Unity's `JsonUtility` class.

Responses can also contain additional HTTP headers. These are the same HTTP headers as for the client/server requests. See `https://developer.mozilla.org/en-US/docs/Web/HTTP/Headers` for more information.

Authentication and Restrictions

You should be respectful of the limits placed by the API provider. They usually limit you to a few hundred calls per minute. More calls than that and you could find yourself banned from the service after repeat offenses.

RESTful API providers also want to ensure that only authorized users have access to their services. This means that you will most likely have to go through some authentication process like *OAuth* or provide a token as part of the URL, typically called an *API token*, that uniquely identifies your application. Tokens usually take the form of a large hexadecimal number:

`42dca02c33584aa783280d83d5e01d04`

The major difference is who owns the authority to use the website. With OAuth, the user must validate themselves to a provider like Google, Facebook, Twitter, or OpenID using a username and password. The result is that they receive a token to use with the remote server. The token is unique to the user.

In the case of the client application owning the authorization, the API key becomes the token. The token is unique to the application.

Note   Always keep tokens and passwords safe! Do not let your token fall into the wrong hands!

In the weather application detailed later in this chapter, you will be using the simpler API token method for OpenWeatherMap rather than OAuth.

The UnityWebRequest Class

Reading and writing data to a remote website is made possible through the UnityWebRequest class. You do not create a UnityWebRequest class directly. Instead you use the Get() method and pass in the URL of the RESTful API endpoint.

The UnityWebRequest class is typically used in a co-routine because of its asynchronous nature. A request is made and at some point in the future that request is given a response.

A normal function in Unity must execute completely before anything else can complete. If there is a function that takes a long time, this will affect the performance of your game. To combat this, Unity created co-routines. These are functions that yield control back to Unity when they need to wait longer than a frame to complete. When the function is called again, it picks up where it left off. See https://docs.unity3d.com/Manual/Coroutines.html for more details.

Errors are handled by checking the isNetworkError and isHttpError properties once the request operation has completed. The text of the error is contained in the error property of the request instance.

The response is located in the text property of the web request's downloadHandler. This is just C# code and no further processing is required. The response will usually be in the JSON format, so creating classes from it is a simple matter of using JsonUtility.FromJson<T>().

Fetching Text

Listing 3-1 illustrates how to fetch a web page. For this example, it's the Google home page. The script can be attached to a game object like the Main Camera in a blank project and run.

Listing 3-1. Fetch the Google Home Page from the Web Using UnityWebRequest

```
using System.Collections;
using UnityEngine;
using UnityEngine.Networking;

public class FetchGoogle : MonoBehaviour
{
    IEnumerator Start()
    {
        UnityWebRequest request = UnityWebRequest.Get(
        "https://www.google.com/");
        yield return request.SendWebRequest();

        if (request.result == UnityWebRequest.Result.Success)
        {
            Debug.Log(request.downloadHandler.text);
        }
        else
        {
            Debug.Log(request.error);
        }
    }
}
```

The Start() method is a co-routine that will not stall out the game while the web request is waiting for a response. The SendWebRequest() method returns an enumerator that exits when either an error occurs or when the data has been received.

If an error occurs in this example, it is printed to the console. If data is returned it is printed to the console, as shown in Figure 3-3. This is the HTML of the Google home page—the one with the search box in the middle of the screen.

Figure 3-3. *The output from the FetchGoogle script showing the contents of the Google home page's HTML*

Note   A request is required for each resource. If you were building a web server, you would have to make several requests for the HTML page, each image, each stylesheet, and each JavaScript file needed to display the page completely.

Fetching Images

The UnityWebRequest class can be used to return an image. The following example fetches the Unity Logo from Wikimedia Commons, as shown in Figure 3-4.

Figure 3-4. *The Unity logo as shown on the Wikimedia Commons website*

Creating the Project

Create the project by completing the following steps:

1. Create a new 2D project from Unity Hub named
    Fetch Example.

2. Add an empty GameObject to the scene called Logo.

3. Add a SpriteRenderer component to the Logo
    GameObject.

4. Create a new folder in Assets called Scripts.

5. Inside the Scripts folder, create a C# script called
    FetchLogo.

6. Attach the FetchLogo script to Logo using the Add
    Component button or by dragging the script onto
    Logo.

The GameObject's component list should look like the one shown in Figure 3-5. Save the scene.

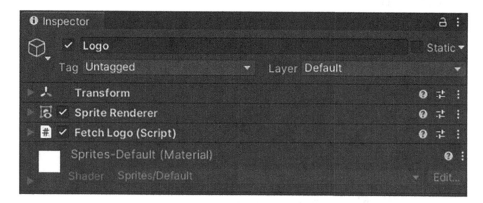

Figure 3-5. *The list of components added to the game object*

Fetching the Image

The UnityWebRequest class is part of a group of classes that are used to download data from remote websites. To download an image, use the UnityWebRequestTexture class.

Open the FetchLogo script and change the script to look like Listing 3-2.

Listing 3-2. Fetching an Image from a Website Using UnityWebRequestTexture

```
using System.Collections;
using UnityEngine;
using UnityEngine.Networking;
```

```
public class FetchLogo : MonoBehaviour
{
    IEnumerator Start()
    {
        string url = "https://upload.wikimedia.org/wikipedia/
        commons/8/8a/Official_unity_logo.png";
        var request = UnityWebRequestTexture.GetTexture(url);

        yield return request.SendWebRequest();
        if (request.result == UnityWebRequest.Result.Success)
        {
            var textureHandler = request.downloadHandler as
            DownloadHandlerTexture;
            Texture2D texture = textureHandler.texture;

            SpriteRenderer = GetComponent<SpriteRenderer>();
            var rect = new Rect(0, 0, texture.width, texture.
            height);
            spriteRenderer.sprite = Sprite.Create(texture,
            rect, Vector2.zero);
        }
        else
        {
            Debug.Log(request.error);
        }
    }
}
```

Instead of using the Get() method, as you did for the text, the GetTexture() method is used. This returns an instance of UnityWebRequestTexture, but, the actual return is an object of type UnityWebRequest. You must do some casting to get the objects back to the type that you need in order to get the texture.

The download handler that is returned from a `UnityWebRequest` is a standard `DownloadHandler` instance. However, after casting the `UnityWebRequestTexture`'s `downloadHandler` property to the `DownloadHandlerTexture` class, we can access the `downloadHandler`'s `texture` property.

Then it is a simple matter of creating a Sprite object and passing the downloaded texture. When run, the image is downloaded and the sprite is constructed, as shown in Figure 3-6.

Figure 3-6. *The Unity logo is displayed in the game after downloading it from the remote site*

Fetching Other Types

Other resources can be downloaded from websites by using the appropriate `UnityWebRequest` class and the associated `DownloadHandler`:

- Audio – `UnityWebRequestMultimedia/DownloadHandler AudioClip`

- Asset Bundle – `UnityWebRequestAssetBundle/Download HandlerAssetBundle`

- Text – `UnityWebRequest/DownloadHandler`

- Textures – `UnityWebRequestTexture/Download HandlerTexture`

Asset bundles can group assets together. Typical uses include texture packs and downloadable content (DLC).

The Weather Application

In this chapter, you are going to build a functioning application that uses data provided by a remote site. Access to the data is through a RESTful API and requires a token.

The *OpenWeather* project provides accurate weather forecasting data and has an API with which to build your own applications. The website, shown in Figure 3-7, is located at `https://openweathermap.org/`.

Figure 3-7. *The OpenWeather home page*

Registering and Getting an API Key

Before you start, you need to obtain an API key. This key will be used in all your queries. To obtain a key, you must first get an account with the site. To do that, locate the Sign In menu option along the top of the page and click the Create an Account link. This will take you to the sign-up page, as shown in Figure 3-8.

Once completed, you will get a confirmation message sent to the email account that you provided. Do not forget to verify your email address!

Note   It can take upwards of two hours to get a confirmation back while OpenWeather creates a valid key.

Figure 3-8. *The OpenWeather sign-up page*

Once logged in, you will be taken to your account home page. Click the API Keys link shown in Figure 3-9.

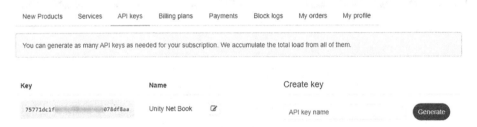

We have sent the confirmation link to **sloankelly** ▓▓▓▓▓▓▓▓▓ Please check your email.

New Products   Services   ⎡ API keys ⎤   Billing plans   Payments   Block logs   My orders   My profile

Historical weather for any location

Figure 3-9. *The API Keys link shown in a box*

By default, an API key is defined for you with the name `default`. You can edit this to be any name you like: for example, the name of your application. The most important part, though, is the key itself. This is what will be used to verify your application when you make a call to an API. Figure 3-10 shows my API key that I have renamed to Unity Net Book. The name is more of a mnemonic for you and is not required when making an API call.

New Products   Services   API keys   Billing plans   Payments   Block logs   My orders   My profile

You can generate as many API keys as needed for your subscription. We accumulate the total load from all of them.

Key	Name	Create key	
75771dc1f▓▓▓▓▓▓▓▓078df8aa	Unity Net Book ✎	API key name	Generate

Figure 3-10. *The default API key has been renamed Unity Net Book*

Note   Each new application requires a different API key.

The User Interface

The application's user interface, shown in Figure 3-11, includes a text box to allow users to enter their city and country, a button to fetch data, and a button to toggle between Celsius and Fahrenheit.

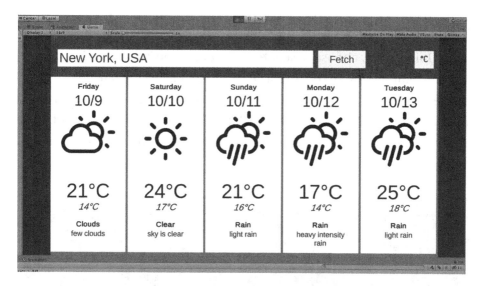

Figure 3-11. *The application showing the five day forecast for New York City*

The resources for this project can be obtained by clicking the Download Source Code button located at www.apress. com/9781484273579. This includes the images for the weather icons, the prefabs for each day, and the fonts.

Creating the Project

Follow these instructions to create the basic WeatherApp project:

1. Create a new blank 2D project in Unity Hub named weather-app.

2. Import the weather-application.unitypackage from the resources folder on the GitHub repo to get the prefabs, images, fonts, and starting scene.

Importing the weather-application.unitypackage

In the Unity editor, choose Assets ➤ Import Package ➤ Custom Package
from the main menu. In the Import Package dialog box, locate the
weather-application.unitypackage and open it. Figure 3-12 shows the
contents of the package. These files will be added to the blank project.
Click Import at the bottom-right side of the dialog to add the files to your
project.

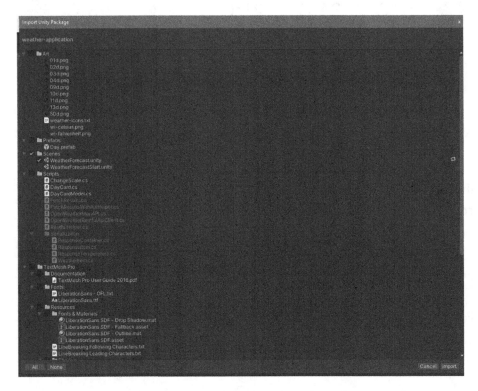

Figure 3-12. *The Import Unity Package window showing the*
contents of the weather-package.unitypackage

The OpenWeather Daily Forecast Endpoint

The OpenWeather daily forecast endpoint allows clients to request up to 16 days of weather from the system. The endpoint documentation is located at https://openweathermap.org/forecast16. The API documentation states that the endpoint is located at:

https://api.openweathermap.org/data/2.5/forecast/daily

The endpoint takes in three parameters that will be passed to the method using an HTTP query string, which you need to provide in order to obtain the data.

A query string is set of key-value pairs that appear after the question mark (?) character in a web address. The key and the value are separated by an equals sign (=). Query strings are not secure because they are part of the web address and are sent in plain text.

The three parameters are:

- q – The city and country code of the location.

- cnt – The number of days to return. You will set this to 5 in your example.

- appid – The API key for the application.

To request the forecast in Boston for the next five days, the URL would look like the following – API key truncated:

https://api.openweathermap.org/data/2.5/forecast/daily?q=Boston
&cnt=5&appid=dc54fac

The API can be tested using the CURL command. Curl stands for *client URL* and is used to download resources from websites on the command line. It's perfect for testing APIs because of this. Open a terminal window or DOS prompt. At the prompt, type in the command like so. Don't forget to change your `appid` to your application's ID:

```
$ curl "https://api.openweathermap.org/data/2.5/forecast/daily?
q=Boston&cnt=5&appid=dc54fac"
```

The query (q) must be URL-encoded. This means that the string will have whitespace characters trimmed out and problematic characters replaced with HTML entities. For example, a space becomes a plus symbol (+). The example shows two lines—the normal text followed by the URL-encoded version:

```
Niagara Falls, Ontario
Niagara+Falls%2c+Ontario
```

The .NET framework's `HttpUtility` class has a method called `UrlEncode()` that will take a string and return the URL-encoded version:

```
var urlEncodedCity = HttpUtility.UrlEncode(city);
```

Fetching the Data

With the barebones project imported via the package, you need to create additional scripts that will:

- Provide classes to decode the JSON message received from the API call

- Use a common function to make the call to the API

- Send out the request when the user clicks the Fetch button

Let's start by creating the script files you need. In the Unity Editor's Project view, open the `Scripts` folder and add the following C# script files:

- `FetchResults`

- `OpenWeatherMapAPI`

Then create a new folder in `Scripts` called `Serialization`. Create the following C# script files inside the `Serialization` folder:

- `ResponseContainer`

- `ResponseItem`

- `ResponseTemperature`

- `WeatherItem`

The last four C# script files will hold the response from the server. You should now have a project that looks like the hierarchy shown in Figure 3-13.

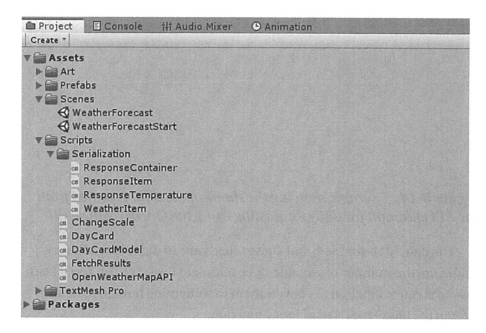

Figure 3-13. *The project hierarchy for the weather application*

Serialization Classes

The serialization classes in `Scripts/Serialization` will just be plain classes with public fields that will be populated with data.

Note   Unity's `JsonUtility` can only serialize/deserialize public fields. Do not use properties for your serialization classes!

The shape of the data (i.e. the names of the fields and the class structure) is dictated by the application. In the case of the daily forecast from OpenWeather, this is defined at `https://openweathermap.org/forecast16#JSON` and a portion of it is shown in Figure 3-14.

Figure 3-14.   *Example showing the shape of the data returned from the API endpoint for daily forecasting using the OpenWeather API*

The date (`dt`), `sunrise`, and `sunset` fields are 10 digits long. These values are the number of seconds since midnight on 1/1/1970. You'll learn how to create a function to convert them to something human readable later in the `UnixTimeToDateTime()` function.

Taking this hierarchy, you can draw a diagram to represent the parent-child relationships of each class as shown in Figure 3-15.

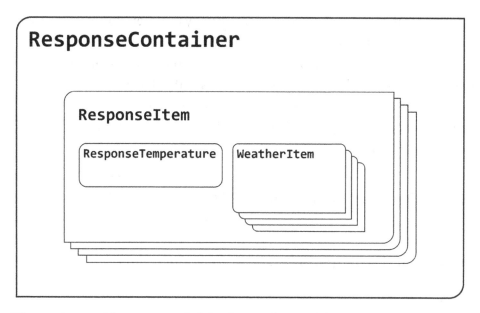

Figure 3-15. *The parent-child relationships of the response message from OpenWeather's API call*

The ResponseContainer is the message received from the server. Each ResponseItem is a day of the week.

The leaf node in this hierarchy is what I called the WeatherItem and it is defined in Listing 3-3.

Listing 3-3. The WeatherItem Script

```
using System;

[Serializable]
public class WeatherItem
{
    public int id;
    public string main;
    public string description;
    public string icon;
}
```

This class contains the icon used to visually represent the weather as well as a description of the weather itself. Paired with the WeatherItem class is the ResponseTemperature class, shown in Listing 3-4. It contains, unsurprisingly, the temperature for the parts of the day. The temperatures returned from the API are in Kelvin. You will write a function called ToHumanTemperature() that will convert the temperature from Kelvin to Celsius or Fahrenheit.

Note   Zero Kelvin is approximately -273 Celsius or -460 Fahrenheit!

Listing 3-4. The ResponseTemperature Script

```
using System;

[Serializable]
public class ResponseTemperature
{
    public float day;
    public float night;
    public float min;
    public float max;
    public float eve;
    public float morn;
}
```

Daily temperatures, icons, and descriptions are contained in the ResponseItem class, as shown in Listing 3-5. This represents a single day's results in addition to the sunrise and sunset times for that day.

Listing 3-5. The ResponseItem Script

```
using System;

[Serializable]
public class ResponseItem
{
    public long dt;
    public ResponseTemperature temp;
    public WeatherItem[] weather;
    public long sunrise;
    public long sunset;
}
```

The dt, sunrise, and sunset fields are not in the DateTime format. This is because the OpenWeatherMap API returns times in what is called UNIX Epoch time. This is the number of seconds since midnight on 1/1/1970.

Lastly, the actual message itself is represented in code as ResponseContainer, as shown in Listing 3-6. It contains a collection of ResponseItem instances as well as the count of the number of days requested.

Listing 3-6. The ResponseContainer Script

```
using System;

[Serializable]
public class ResponseContainer
{
    public string cod;
    public float message;
    public int cnt;
    public ResponseItem[] list;
}
```

Now that the serializable classes have been defined, you can take a look at creating a MonoBehaviour that queries the OpenWeather endpoint for a particular location and returns the result to the caller.

Calling the API

As in the previous examples, you will use the UnityWebRequest class to fetch the data from the remote server. JsonUtility.FromJson<T>() is used to create the ResponseContainer from the JSON response.

There is one exposed field that is settable through the Unity editor for the API key. You will have to provide that key yourself. The entire class is shown in Listing 3-7.

Listing 3-7. The OpenWeatherMapAPI MonoBehaviour Script

```
using System.Collections;
using System.Web;
using UnityEngine;
using UnityEngine.Networking;

public class OpenWeatherMapAPI : MonoBehaviour
{
    private static readonly string ApiBaseUrl =
    "https://api.openweathermap.org/data/2.5/forecast/
    daily?q={0}&cnt=5&appid={1}";

    [Tooltip("The key that allows access to the OpenWeatherMap API")]
    public string apiKey;

    public ResponseContainer Response { get; private set; }

    public IEnumerator GetForecast(string city)
    {
        Response = null;
        string urlEncodedCity = HttpUtility.UrlEncode(city);
```

```
    string url = string.Format(ApiBaseUrl, urlEncodedCity,
    apiKey);
    UnityWebRequest webRequest = UnityWebRequest.Get(url);
    yield return webRequest.SendWebRequest();

    if (webRequest.result == UnityWebRequest.Result.Success)
    {
        string json = webRequest.downloadHandler.text;
        Response = JsonUtility.FromJson<ResponseContainer>(
        json);
    }
    else
    {
        Debug.Log(webRequest.error);
    }
  }
}
```

Notice that the endpoint is stored as a constant called `ApiBaseUrl` and the `string.Format()` method is used to place the query and the API key in the query. Also of note is the `UrlEncode()` method, which is used to encode the query string.

This `MonoBehaviour` is used by the final script that you write, which acts as a controller for the whole application. If you were writing an application that uses a lot of API calls, it would be rather inefficient to rewrite this over and over again. At the end of this chapter, you'll take a look at making this more generic.

The Controller: Final Wiring

The controller acts as the glue code between the UI and the API. The script is attached to the `FetchButton` object in the project hierarchy, shown in Figure 3-16, along with the `OpenWeatherMapAPI MonoBehaviour`.

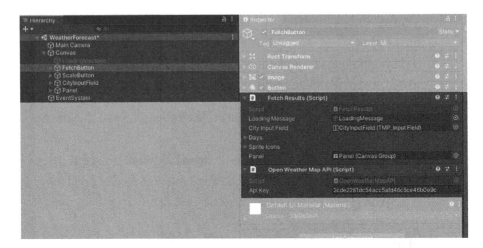

Figure 3-16. *The FetchButton GameObject with the two script components: FetchResults and OpenWeatherMapAPI*

The FetchResults class, as shown in Listing 3-8, adds a click event handler to the button to which it is attached. The event handler calls the FetchData() method and that in turn calls the OpenWeatherMapAPI's GetForecast() method. On a successful response, the day prefabs are filled.

Listing 3-8. The FetchResults MonoBehaviour script

```
using System.Collections;
using System.Collections.Generic;
using TMPro;
using UnityEngine;
using UnityEngine.UI;

public class FetchResults : MonoBehaviour
{
    private static readonly string DefaultIcon = "01d";

    private bool isRunningQuery;
```

```
private Button;
private OpenWeatherMapAPI api;
private Dictionary<string, Sprite> sprites = new
Dictionary<string, Sprite>();

public GameObject loadingMessage;
public TMP_InputField cityInputField;
public DayCard[] dayCards;

public Sprite[] spriteIcons;

public CanvasGroup panel;

void Awake()
{
    button = GetComponent<Button>();
    api = GetComponent<OpenWeatherMapAPI>();

    // Create the dictionary that maps the name of the
    sprite to its image
    foreach (Sprite s in spriteIcons)
    {
        sprites[s.name] = s;
    }

    button.onClick.AddListener(delegate
    {
        if (!string.IsNullOrEmpty(cityInputField.text.
        Trim()) && !isRunningQuery)
        {
            StartCoroutine(FetchData(cityInputField.text));
        }
    });
}
```

```
private IEnumerator FetchData(string query)
{
    isRunningQuery = true;
    panel.alpha = 0;
    loadingMessage.SetActive(true);
    yield return api.GetForecast(query);
    loadingMessage.SetActive(false);
    isRunningQuery = false;

    if (api.Response != null)
    {
        FillDays(api.Response);
        panel.alpha = 1;
    }
}

private void FillDays(ResponseContainer response)
{
    panel.alpha = 1;

    for (int i = 0; i < dayCards.Length; i++)
    {
        var icon = response.list[i].weather[0].icon;
        if (!sprites.ContainsKey(icon))
        {
            icon = DefaultIcon;
        }

        Sprite = sprites[icon];
        DayCardModel day = new DayCardModel(response.
        list[i], sprite);
        DayCard = dayCards[i];
```

```
            dayCard.SetModel(day);
        }
    }
}
```

The final thing to do is to enter the API token on the `OpenWeatherMapAPI` script in the Unity Editor. At this point, you can test the application—everything is complete!

Running the Weather Application

Save all the open code files in your editor/IDE. In the Unity Editor, click the Play button to start the app. Enter your location in the text box and click the Fetch button. You should see the days appear. If not, here are some things to check:

- The code is typed exactly as written
- You have a network connection
- You have entered the API token correctly
- Your token is valid

Remember that it can take up to two hours for the token to be validated by the `OpenWeather` service. Check your email!

Generic RESTful API Client

As I mentioned earlier, you may find yourself doing multiple calls to various endpoints to build your client. If this is the case, it is better to abstract the remote call out of the class and into a helper class.

Listing 3-9 shows how this can be achieved using a static method on a static class. The RestfulHelper class' Fetch method takes three parameters:

- endPoint – The endpoint of the API method

- onSuccess – An action to be called when the data has been successfully received by the client

- onError – An action to be called when the data could not be retrieved by the client

The helper class also correctly handles the disposal of the UnityWebRequest class by wrapping it inside a using block.

Listing 3-9. The RestfulHelper Class

```
using System;
using System.Collections;
using UnityEngine;
using UnityEngine.Networking;

public static class RestfulHelper
{
    public static IEnumerator Fetch<T>(string endPoint,
    Action<T> onSuccess, Action<string> onError) where T:
    class, new()
    {
        using (UnityWebRequest webRequest = UnityWebRequest.
        Get(endPoint))
        {
            yield return webRequest.SendWebRequest();

            if (webRequest.isNetworkError || webRequest.
            isHttpError)
            {
```

```
            onError?.Invoke(webRequest.error);
        }
        else
        {
            string json = webRequest.downloadHandler.text;
            onSuccess?.Invoke(JsonUtility.
            FromJson<T>(json));
        }
    }
  }
}
```

The OpenWeatherMapAPI class can now be rewritten (see Listing 3-10) to take advantage of this new helper class. Any additional endpoint calls can be defined in this class and called each from a separate method. Because you're calling only one endpoint, you use GetForecast(), but you could add other methods, like GetDailyForecast(), GetGlobalAlerts(), etc.

Listing 3-10. The Refactored OpenWeatherMapAPI Class Utilizing the RestfulHelper Static Class

```
using System;
using System.Collections;
using System.Web;
using UnityEngine;

class OpenWeatherMapAPI : MonoBehaviour
{
    private static readonly string ApiBaseUrl =
    "https://api.openweathermap.org/data/2.5/forecast/
    daily?q={0}&cnt=5&appid={1}";

    [Tooltip("The key that allows access to the OpenWeatherMap API")]
    public string apiKey;
```

87

```
public IEnumerator GetForecast(string city,
Action<ResponseContainer> onSuccess)
{
    string urlEncodedCity = HttpUtility.UrlEncode(city);
    string url = string.Format(ApiBaseUrl, urlEncodedCity,
    apiKey);
    yield return RestfulHelper.Fetch(url, onSuccess, print);
}
}
```

With the signature of GetForecast() changing, Action<Response Container> has been added as a required parameter. You must also change the FetchResults.FetchData() method, as shown in Listing 3-11.

Listing 3-11. The Modified FetchData() Method in the FetchResults Class

```
private IEnumerator FetchData(string query)
{
    runningQuery = true;
    panel.alpha = 0;
    loadingMessage.SetActive(true);
    yield return api.GetForecast(query, FillDays);
    loadingMessage.SetActive(false);
    runningQuery = false;
}
```

The bold code line is the one that performs the API call to get the forecast data. The FillDays() method will be called automatically once the remote call has completed successfully.

Summary

Your game can act as a client to a remote service that exposes various methods using a RESTful interface. This will allow you to perform read and write operations on remote data. These are performed by requesting a particular URL or endpoint.

There are two methods of authentication: one is per user, the other is per application. OAuth requires users to sign in to a service like Google, Twitter, etc. and obtain a token. The alternative is that the application provides the token. The token is then passed via each call to the remote server to validate the request. Out of date or invalid tokens will get rejected.

Results from the remote service are usually returned in a JSON format. Classes can be easily created using the JSON function built into Unity.

If you are making multiple calls to different endpoints, it is a good idea to create a generic function to perform the remote calls.

The weather application uses a high-level client server architecture. It's now time to switch gears and look at the lower-level socket programming that is provided as part of the .NET framework, as this will allow you to create your own protocols.

CHAPTER 4

TCP Connections

In Chapter 3, you used the `UnityWebRequest` class as a client to access data stored on a website (the server). The `UnityWebRequest` class handled all the underlying communication with the web server. This included the use of HTTP (HyperText Transport Protocol) to format messages and deconstruct the data returned from the server.

HTTP is quite a heavy protocol and is not recommended for games beyond its use at fetching leaderboards, or for updating a player's save game to a cloud service. This chapter looks at how you can create your own protocol that will provide a client/server game; you will use Transport Control Protocol (TCP) to do that.

Remember that TCP is a connection-oriented protocol. This means that the messages that are passed to and from the client and server are in order and complete. All of this is handled at the TCP level; how it achieves the connection and maintains the integrity of the data is determined by the way the client and server synchronize and acknowledge data.

The TCP Three-Way Handshake

TCP is a connection-oriented protocol and, as such, it has a way of tracking and ensuring that data that's sent is received by the remote party. It does this using a system called *sequence and acknowledgement numbers*.

© Sloan Kelly and Khagendra Kumar 2022
S. Kelly and K. Kumar, *Unity Networking Fundamentals*,
https://doi.org/10.1007/978-1-4842-7358-6_4

- The client establishes a connection with the remote machine. It sends a synchronization message (SYN) with a sequence number and lets the remote machine know that the client is ready.

- The server responds to the client with a synchronization/acknowledgement (SYN-ACK). The ACK contains the next number in the client's SYN message and the SYN holds the sequence number to start subsequent messages.

- The client acknowledges (ACK) the response of the server with the next number in the server's SYN message.

The three-way handshake is complete, so the local machine (client) and the remote machine (server) can begin the actual data transfer process. This is illustrated in Figure 4-1.

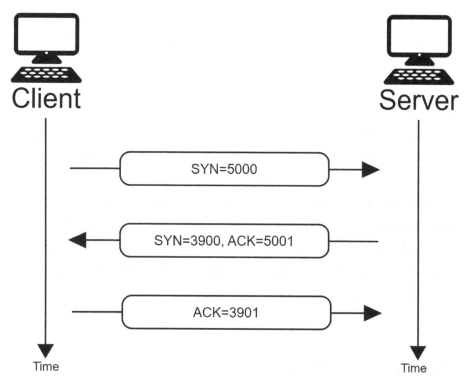

Figure 4-1. *The TCP three-way handshake illustrating the SYN/ACK sequence numbers*

TCP Client-Server Connections

The TcpListener class in the System.Net.Sockets namespace provides you with a simple way to allow incoming TCP connections to be established in your game. The TcpListener can accept an incoming *socket* or *TcpClient*. It provides both synchronous and asynchronous methods to accept connections.

Once a server is created, a remote machine can try to connect to it. These requests will be placed in a queue that is handled by the underlying networking framework. This isn't something you have to worry about!

However, be careful when using synchronous calls. When there is nothing in the queue, the main thread will be blocked, waiting for clients to connect or messages to be received.

Note   Synchronous method calls are blocking calls. This means that the main thread cannot do anything while waiting for the method to return a value or complete the task. On the other hand, asynchronous calls allow you to provide a callback (another method to call) when something happens. Think of them as event-driven network programming. Asynchronous calls allow the main thread to keep processing—moving characters around, updating animations, and so on. The downside is that messages received are on another thread. This will be covered later.

Socket Connections

Remember that Berkeley's networking suite abstracted network programming using the file descriptor paradigm. A socket is a file descriptor for networking and it represents an IP address and a port number. Any communication to and from the remote server can be made through the Socket class.

A connection to a remote server can be made using the low-level Socket class. Because this class is IDisposable, I recommend wrapping it inside a using(), as shown in Listing 4-1.

Listing 4-1. Creating a TCP Socket Wrapped Inside a using() Block

```
using (var socket = new Socket(SocketType.Stream,
ProtocolType.Tcp))
{
    // Send and receive and then close the socket
    socket.Close();
}
```

The socket type and protocol are passed to the socket in the constructor. The socket type is Stream. This represents a connection-oriented service and the protocol type is TCP because that is the protocol you are using to establish the connection.

Note   You should always call Close() on a Socket class.

Establishing a Socket Connection

To connect to a remote server, use the Connect() method. It takes two parameters. The first is the IP address of the remote server and the second is the port where the service is running. Listing 4-2 shows that the client is connecting to a service running on the local machine at port 9021.

Listing 4-2. Connecting to a Local Service Running on Port 9021

```
try
{
    socket.Connect(IPAddress.Parse("127.0.0.1"), 9021);
}
catch (SocketException e)
{
    print(e);
}
```

Because the Connect() method can throw an exception, it is best to wrap it inside a try/catch block, as shown in this example.

Accepting a Socket Connection

There are two ways to accept an incoming socket connection using TcpListener—AcceptSocket(), which is synchronous and BeginAcceptSocket(), which is asynchronous.

Listing 4-3 shows how to accept a socket connection synchronously. We will not be using this method in the book. This is a blocking call and it's best not to block the main thread.

Listing 4-3. Accepting a Socket Synchronously

```
var listener = new TcpListener(IPAddress.Any, 9021);
listener.Start()
Socket = listener.AcceptSocket();
```

The better option is to use the BeginAcceptSocket() method, which takes two parameters:

- The callback method

- The state object

The state object can be anything or null, but I recommend passing in the listener. It will be accessible through the callback's IAsyncResult parameter's AsyncState property.

Listing 4-4 shows how to create a TcpListener instance listening on port 9021 of the local machine using any IP and to signal when a connection from a remote machine has been established.

Listing 4-4. Accepting a Socket Connection Asynchronously

```
var listener = new TcpListener(IPAddress.Any, 9021);
listener.Start();
listener.BeginAcceptSocket(Socket_Connected, _listener);
```

Listing 4-5 shows the code for the Socket_Connected event. Notice that the AsyncState is accessed as a TcpListener because that is the state object that you passed into the BeginAcceptSocket() call.

Listing 4-5. Completing the Acceptance of an Incoming Socket Connection

```
private void Socket_Connected(IAsyncResult ar)
{
    if (ar.IsCompleted)
    {
        var socket = (ar.AsyncState as TcpListener)
                    .EndAcceptSocket(ar);
        // TO DO: Do something with socket
    }
}
```

Sending Data

Data is sent to the remote server using Send() or BeginSend(). The Send() method is the synchronous call and BeginSend() is the asynchronous call.

As with all data transferred via sockets, it takes the form of a byte array. Byte arrays will form part of your serialization/deserialization routines. For now, though, these examples will just use plain ASCII text converted to and from a byte array.

Synchronous Send

Listing 4-6 illustrates how to send a simple ASCII message to the remote server using a byte[] array.

Listing 4-6. Sending a Simple Message Using a Blocking Call

```
byte[] msgOut = Encoding.ASCII.GetBytes("Hello, World!");
int bytesOut = socket.Send(msgOut);
```

The number of bytes sent is returned from the Send() method. If the number of bytes sent is less than the total number of bytes in your message, you will have to advance the pointer and send again. A simple while loop can be used, as shown in Listing 4-7. The receiver will also have a buffer to accept the incoming data. The receiver will have to maintain a count of received bytes to make sure that the complete message has been received. The buffer can be periodically written out to disk or some other storage—a memory stream for example.

Listing 4-7. Sending a Large Amount of Data in Multiple Sends

```
int sizeOfBuffer = buffer.Length;
int offset = 0;
int sent = socket.Send(buffer,
                       offset,
                       buffer.Length,
                       SocketFlags.None);
while (sent < sizeOfBuffer)
{
    sizeOfBuffer = Mathf.Max(0, sizeOfBuffer - sent);
    offset += sent;
```

```
sent = socket.Send(buffer,
                   offset,
                   buffer.Length - offset,
                   SocketFlags.None);
}
```

The Send() method in Listing 4-7 takes four parameters:

- The buffer containing the message to send

- The offset inside the buffer to send

- The size of the message to send

- Socket flags

The offset is used to point to the next element in the array to start sending the data from. For example, if you have a buffer of 100 bytes and send 10 bytes at a time, the offset will be set to 0, 10, 20, 30, and so on, as each part of the buffer is filled and sent to the receiver.

Asynchronous Send

Sending data asynchronously is achieved through the BeginSend() method. The asynchronous callback takes an IAsyncResult object that contains an AsyncState property. This property can be filled by passing the state parameter to BeginState(). I recommend that you pass in the socket, as shown in Listing 4-8.

Listing 4-8. Asynchronous Sending of Data Using a TCP Socket

```
void Start()
{
    var socket = new Socket(SocketType.Stream,
                            ProtocolType.Tcp);
    socket.Connect(IPAddress.Parse("127.0.0.1"), 9021);
```

```
    var msg = Encoding.ASCII.GetBytes("Hello, from Client!");
    socket.BeginSend(msg,
                     0,
                     msg.Length,
                     SocketFlags.None,
                     Send_Complete,
                     socket);
}

void Send_Complete(IAsyncResult ar)
{
    if (ar.IsCompleted)
    {
        var socket = ar.AsyncState as Socket;
        var bytesSent = socket.EndSend(ar);
        print($"{bytesSent} bytes sent");
    }
}
```

The BeginSend() method takes six parameters:

- The buffer containing the message to send

- The offset inside the buffer to send

- The length of the message

- Socket flags

- The asynchronous result callback

- The state object

Note   The state object can be null, but for BeginSend(), I recommend using the Socket instance.

Receiving Data

Data is received by both the client and the server; the client when receiving a result from the server and the server when receiving a request from the client. In order to receive data from a remote machine, you must have a place to store the incoming messages. In C#, this is a byte array.

As with sending, you can receive synchronously with the Receive() method and asynchronously with the BeginReceive() method.

Synchronous Receive

Listing 4-9 illustrates how to receive a message into a buffer using a socket. The code assumes that socket is a valid instance of Socket.

Listing 4-9. Receiving Data Into a Buffer from a Remote Machine Using a Socket

```
byte[] buffer = new byte[1024];
var bytesReceived = socket.Receive(buffer);
var recv = Encoding.ASCII.GetString(buffer, 0, bytesReceived);
print(recv);
```

Receiving a larger file into a smaller buffer is possible. It is good practice for the sender to send information about the data being transferred, including the size of the file. If you were going to write a file transfer program, you might want to send the size of the file as the first part of the transmission and then the contents of the file as the remainder.

The receiver would then read the first four bytes and use this as a counter against the number of bytes received. Listing 4-10 contains code that receives a byte array. The first four bytes represent an integer indicating the size of the transfer. BitConverter.ToInt32() can convert bytes to an integer easily and the remaining bytes of the message are a matter of arithmetic.

Listing 4-10. Receiving a Large File Over TCP Using a Socket

```
byte[] superBuffer;
var buffer = new byte[1024];

var recv = client.Receive(buffer);
int length = BitConverter.ToInt32(buffer, 0);
superBuffer = new byte[length];

recv -= 4;
int sbOffset = recv;
int bytesRemaining = length - recv;
Array.Copy(buffer, 4, superBuffer, 0, sbOffset);
while (bytesRemaining > 0)
{
    Array.Clear(buffer, 0, buffer.Length);
    recv = client.Receive(buffer);
    bytesRemaining -= recv;

    Array.Copy(buffer, 0, superBuffer, sbOffset, recv);
    sbOffset += recv;
}
```

This is part of a program that receives a file sent over the network. The first four bytes of a received file is the length of the file. These four bytes are converted into an integer and the remaining bytes are added to a buffer that will contain the whole file.

Messages are received into a temporary byte array that's 1024 bytes in size, called *buffer*. The *superBuffer* is created with the length of the actual file—the first four bytes of the received data. The contents of buffer are copied to *superBuffer*. This process is repeated until there are no more bytes to copy, i.e., bytesRemaining is zero.

Asynchronous Receive

As with the synchronous Receive(), any messages received will go into a buffer. Because there is a callback involved, it would be difficult to access this buffer if it was created locally. Therefore, I recommend creating a state object that can be used to hold not only the socket that sent the message but also the buffer. Listing 4-11 shows such a class.

Listing 4-11. An Example State Object with Socket and Buffer Properties

```
using System.Net.Sockets;

public class StateObject
{
    public byte[] Buffer { get; }
    public Socket Socket { get; }

    public StateObject(Socket socket, int bufferSize = 1024)
    {
        Buffer = new byte[bufferSize];
        Socket = socket;
    }
}
```

The StateObject can be used to pass information to the callback through the IAsyncResult.AsyncState property. For example, when a socket connects, you can start to receive on that socket, as shown in Listing 4-12.

Listing 4-12. The Socket_Connected Callback Sets Up an Asynchronous Receive

```
private void Socket_Connected(IAsyncResult ar)
{
    if (ar.IsCompleted)
    {
        var socket = (ar.AsyncState as TcpListener)
                    .EndAcceptSocket(ar);
        var state = new StateObject(socket);
        socket.BeginReceive(state.Buffer,
                            0,
                            state.Buffer.Length,
                            SocketFlags.None,
                            Socket_Received,
                            state);
    }
}
```

The BeginReceive() method takes six parameters:

- The buffer that the message will be received into

- The offset inside this buffer

- The number of bytes that can be received

- Socket flags

- The received callback

- The state object

The received callback is called when the operation completes. Listing 4-13 shows how to complete a receive.

Listing 4-13. Completing a Receive on a TCP Socket

```
private void Socket_Received(IAsyncResult ar)
{
    if (ar.IsCompleted)
    {
        var state = ar.AsyncState as StateObject;
        var bytesIn = state.Socket.EndReceive(ar);

        var newState = new StateObject(state.Socket);
        state.Socket.BeginReceive(state.Buffer,
                                  0,
                                  state.Buffer.Length,
                                  SocketFlags.None,
                                  Socket_Received,
                                  newState);
    }
}
```

Once you have completed a receive, you must call BeginReceive() again if you want to allow the client to send you multiple messages or if you have not received the correct number of bytes in a larger message. The number of bytes received is returned in bytesIn. Check this variable. You may have to go through a loop like in Listing 4-10.

Hello World Using TCP Sockets

In this example, you will create a Unity project that re-creates the classic "Hello, World" program, but using TcpListener and Socket. To create this project, follow these steps:

1. Create a new 2D project in Unity.

2. Create a Scripts folder inside the Assets folder.

3. Create a C# script file called
   `TcpSocketAsyncBehaviour` inside the `Scripts`
   folder.

4. Create a C# script file called
   `TcpListenSocketBehaviour` inside the `Scripts`
   folder.

5. Create a C# script file called `StateObject` inside the
   `Scripts` folder.

6. Drag and drop the `TcpListenSocketBehaviour`
   script onto the `MainCamera` in the scene view.

7. Drag and drop the `TcpSocketAsyncBehaviour` onto
   the `MainCamera` in the scene view.

8. Save the scene as `AsyncSockets`.

You should now have a project hierarchy like the one shown in
Figure 4-2.

Figure 4-2. *The hierarchy of the Async Sockets project*

Open the `StateObject` script file in your IDE and change the text to the
contents of Listing 4-14. Make sure you save this file when you're done.

Listing 4-14. The StateObject Script File

```
using System.Net.Sockets;

public class StateObject
{
    public byte[] Buffer { get; }
    public Socket Socket { get; }

    public StateObject(Socket socket, int bufferSize = 1024)
    {
        Buffer = new byte[bufferSize];
        Socket = socket;
    }
}
```

The StateObject class is used by the TcpListenSocketBehaviour
class. Open the TcpListenSocketBehaviour script file in your IDE and
change the text to the contents of Listing 4-15. Save the file when you are
done.

Listing 4-15. The TcpListenSocketBehaviour Script File

```
using System;
using System.Net;
using System.Net.Sockets;
using System.Text;
using UnityEngine;

public class TcpListenSocketBehaviour : MonoBehaviour
{
    private TcpListener _listener;

    [HideInInspector]
    public bool _isReady;
```

```csharp
[Tooltip("The port the service is running on")]
public int _port = 9021;

void Start()
{
    _listener = new TcpListener(IPAddress.Any, _port);
    _listener.Start();
    _listener.BeginAcceptSocket(Socket_Connected,
                                _listener);

    _isReady = true;
}
private void OnDestroy()
{
    _listener?.Stop();
    _listener = null;
}

private void Socket_Connected(IAsyncResult ar)
{
    if (ar.IsCompleted)
    {
        var socket = (ar.AsyncState as TcpListener)
                    .EndAcceptSocket(ar);
        var state = new StateObject(socket);

        socket.BeginReceive(state.Buffer,
                            0,
                            state.Buffer.Length,
                            SocketFlags.None,
                            Socket_Received,
                            state);
    }
}
```

```csharp
private void Socket_Received(IAsyncResult ar)
{
    if (ar.IsCompleted)
    {
        var state = ar.AsyncState as StateObject;
        var bytesIn = state.Socket.EndReceive(ar);

        if (bytesIn > 0)
        {
            var msg = Encoding.ASCII
                            .GetString(state.Buffer,
                                        0,
                                        bytesIn);
            print($"From client: {msg}");
        }

        var newState = new StateObject(state.Socket);
        state.Socket.BeginReceive(state.Buffer,
                                0,
                                state.Buffer.Length,
                                SocketFlags.None,
                                Socket_Received,
                                newState);
    }
}
}
```

Finally, TcpSocketAsyncBehaviour is shown in Listing 4-16. Open the TcpSocketAsyncBehaviour script file and enter the text in Listing 4-16. Save the file when you're done.

Listing 4-16. The TcpSocketAsyncBehaviour Script

```
using System;
using System.Collections;
using System.Net;
using System.Net.Sockets;
using System.Text;
using UnityEngine;

[RequireComponent(typeof(TcpListenSocketBehaviour))]
public class TcpSocketAsyncBehaviour : MonoBehaviour
{
    private Socket _socket;

    [Tooltip("The port the service is running on")]
    public int _port = 9021;

    IEnumerator Start()
    {
        var listener =
                    GetComponent<TcpListenSocketBehaviour>();
        while (!listener._isReady)
        {
            yield return null;
        }
        _socket = new Socket(SocketType.Stream,
                            ProtocolType.Tcp);
        _socket.Connect(IPAddress.Parse("127.0.0.1"), _port);
        var msg = Encoding.ASCII.GetBytes("Hello, from Client!");
        _socket.BeginSend(msg,
                        0,
                        msg.Length,
                        SocketFlags.None,
```

```
                         Send_Complete,
                         _socket);
    }

    private void Send_Complete(IAsyncResult ar)
    {
        if (ar.IsCompleted)
        {
            var socket = ar.AsyncState as Socket;
            var bytesSent = socket.EndSend(ar);
            print($"{bytesSent} bytes sent");
        }
    }
}
```

Check your typing and save the files if you haven't already. Run the program. The TcpListenSocketBehaviour is the server. It is waiting for a socket to connect to it and begin communications. The TcpSocketAsyncBehaviour is the client. It connects to the server and sends a simple "Hello, from Client!" message.

The message is converted to a byte array and sent to the server using TCP. It is received and placed in a local byte buffer. The text can be extracted from this byte array and displayed onscreen, as shown in Figure 4-3.

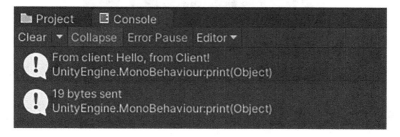

Figure 4-3. *The output from the Async Sockets Unity project*

Simple Network Copier

To illustrate a synchronous network call, I created a program that can copy a file from the local machine to a remote device. I have found this handy when I want to copy files from one computer to another, but I don't want to set up an FTP server or network share.

This is a command-line tool, but it's easily something that could be adapted to Unity if you needed this functionality. To create the project, follow these steps:

1. Create a new Console application in Visual Studio using the latest .net framework.

2. Create a class file called Config.cs.

3. Create a class file called Receiver.cs.

4. Create a class file called Sender.cs.

Along with Program.cs, you should now have the same solution hierarchy as shown in Figure 4-4. The names of the solution file and project might be different; the ones in the figure are NetCopy and ncp respectively, but that won't matter.

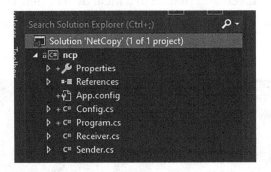

Figure 4-4. *The network copier project hierarchy*

This is a command-line tool. You have to open a DOS/command prompt to run these. To run the program as a server (receiving a file), use the following command-line format. The filename is required. This is the destination filename that the file will be copied into.

```
$ ncp -p 9021 mypicture.png
```

The port option can be omitted. It defaults to the 9021 port if not specified:

```
$ ncp mypicture.png
```

To send a file, the following command-line format is used:

```
$ ncp -ip 127.0.0.1 -port 9021 mypicture.png
```

The IP is the IP address of the server. The port is the port number the service is running on. The last parameter is the local file to copy to the remote server.

The first class you will look at is the Config class. This class parses the command-line arguments for the following parameters:

- Filename
- Port (default is 9021)
- IsServer (default is True)
- Debug (Boolean)
- ServerIP (default is IPAddress.Any)
- AskForHelp (Boolean)

Open the Config.cs file and enter the code in Listing 4-17; save the file.

Listing 4-17. The Config Command-Line Parser

```
using System.Linq;
using System.Net;

namespace SloanKelly.Networking.NetCopy
{
    class Config
    {
        public string Filename { get; }

        public int Port { get; } = 9021;

        public bool IsServer { get; } = true;

        public bool Debug { get; }

        public IPAddress ServerIP { get; }

        public bool AskForHelp { get; }

        public Config(string[] args)
        {
            ServerIP = IPAddress.Any;

            if (args.Length ==0)
            {
                return;
            }

            int index = 0;
            while (index < args.Length)
            {
                if (IsMatch(args[index], "-ip", "/ip", "ip"))
                {
                    index++;
```

```
            ServerIP = IPAddress.Parse(args[index]);
            IsServer = false;
        } else if (IsMatch(args[index], "-p", "/p",
        "port"))
        {
            index++;
            Port = int.Parse(args[index]);
        }
        else if (IsMatch(args[index], "-h", "/h", "/
        help", "help"))
        {
            AskForHelp = true;
            return;
        }
        else if(IsMatch(args[index], "-d", "/d"))
        {
            Debug = true;
        }
        else
        {
            Filename = args[index];
        }

        index++;
    }
}

private bool IsMatch(string leftHand, params string[]
rightHand)
{
    var match = rightHand.FirstOrDefault(s => s ==
    leftHand.ToLower());
```

```
            return !string.IsNullOrEmpty(match);
        }
    }
}
```

The Sender class sends the file to the remote machine. It does this by reading in the contents of a file as a byte array and sending that byte array to the server. Before it sends the contents of the file, it sends an integer (four bytes). This integer contains the length of the file. This is important because the server has no idea how large the payload is until you tell it.

Note   Protocols are all about setting up rules, such as "The first four bytes represent the size of the file being sent."

Open the Sender.cs file and enter the code in Listing 4-18. Save the file when you're done.

Listing 4-18. The Sender Class Used to Send Data to a Remote Server

```
using System;
using System.IO;
using System.Net;
using System.Net.Sockets;

namespace SloanKelly.Networking.NetCopy
{
    class Sender
    {
        private IPAddress _serverIP;
        private int _port;
        private string _filename;
        private bool _debug;
```

```csharp
public Sender(IPAddress serverIP, int port, string
filename, bool debug)
{
    _serverIP = serverIP;
    _port = port;
    _filename = filename;
    _debug = debug;
}

public void Run()
{
    var contents = File.ReadAllBytes(_filename);
    var offset = 0;
    var length = contents.Length;

    var socket = Create(_serverIP, _port);
    if (socket == null)
        return;

    socket.Send(BitConverter.GetBytes(contents.Length));

    while (length > 0)
    {
        var sent = socket.Send(contents,
                                offset,
                                length,
                                SocketFlags.None);
        length -= sent;
        offset += sent;
        Console.WriteLine($"Sent {sent} byte(s)");
        socket.Send(contents,
                    offset,
                    length,
                    SocketFlags.None);
    }
```

```
            Console.WriteLine("Finished!");
            socket.Close();
            socket.Dispose();
        }

        private Socket Create(IPAddress ip, int port)
        {
            try
            {
                var socket = new Socket(SocketType.Stream,
                                        ProtocolType.Tcp);
                socket.Connect(ip, port);
                return socket;
            }
            catch (Exception e)
            {
                Console.WriteLine(e);
            }

            return null;
        }
    }
}
```

The Receiver class receives the data from the remote client. As discussed, it uses two buffers. The first is the main buffer used to store the entire file. The second is a smaller receive buffer, which is 1KB (1024 bytes) in size.

Open the Receiver.cs file in the IDE and enter the code from Listing 4-19. Save the file when you're done.

Listing 4-19. The Receiver Class Is Used to Receive the Data

```
using System;
using System.IO;
using System.Net;
using System.Net.Sockets;

namespace SloanKelly.Networking.NetCopy
{
    class Receiver
    {
        private IPAddress _serverIP;
        private int _port;
        private string _fileName;
        private bool _debug;
        public Receiver(IPAddress serverIP, int port, string
        fileName, bool debug)
        {
            _serverIP = serverIP;
            _port = port;
            _fileName = fileName;
            _debug = debug;
        }

        public void Run()
        {
            Console.WriteLine("Listening for connection");
            var contents = ReceiveContents();

            if (contents == null || contents.Length == 0)
            {
                return;
            }
```

```
    else
    {
        File.WriteAllBytes(_fileName, contents);
    }
}

private byte[] ReceiveContents()
{
    byte[] superBuffer;

    var listener = new TcpListener(_serverIP, _port);
    listener.Start();
    var socket = listener.AcceptSocket();

    var buffer = new byte[1024];
    var recv = socket.Receive(buffer);
    recv -= 4;
    int length = BitConverter.ToInt32(buffer, 0);
    superBuffer = new byte[length];

    Console.WriteLine($"Size of file received is
    {length} byte(s)");

    if (_debug)
        Console.WriteLine($"Received {recv} byte(s)");

    int sbOffset = recv;
    int bytesRemaining = length - recv;
    Array.Copy(buffer, 4, superBuffer, 0, sbOffset);
    while (bytesRemaining > 0)
    {
        Array.Clear(buffer, 0, buffer.Length);
        recv = socket.Receive(buffer);
```

```
        bytesRemaining -= recv;
        if (_debug)
            Console.WriteLine($"Received {recv}
            byte(s). {bytesRemaining} left.");
        Array.Copy(buffer,
                    0,
                    superBuffer,
                    sbOffset,
                    recv);
        sbOffset += recv;
    }

    socket.Close();
    socket.Dispose();
    listener.Stop();

    return superBuffer;
        }
    }
}
```

Lastly is the Program class. This is the entry point into the application. It creates the classes that will be used, depending on the contents of the arguments passed on the command line. These are parsed out using the Config class. Help is given if the user requests it or if they make an error in the arguments passed.

Open the Program.cs file and enter the code in Listing 4-20. Save the file when you're done.

Listing 4-20. Program Is the Entry Point to the Application

```
using System;

namespace SloanKelly.Networking.NetCopy
{
    class Program
    {
        static void Main(string[] args)
        {
            var config = new Config(args);
            if (config.AskForHelp || string.
            IsNullOrEmpty(config.Filename))
            {
                Console.WriteLine("NetCopy - Sloan Kelly 2020");
                Console.WriteLine("Provides a simple peer to
                peer copy from one machine to another");
                Console.WriteLine("Usage");
                Console.WriteLine("\tSend\tncp [-ip serverIP]
                [-p port] filename");
                Console.WriteLine("\tReceive\tncp [-p port]
                filename");
            }
            else if (config.IsServer)
            {
                var server = new Receiver(config.ServerIP,
                                          config.Port,
                                          config.Filename,
                                          config.Debug);

                server.Run();
            }
```

```
        else
        {
            var sender = new Sender(config.ServerIP,
                                    config.Port,
                                    config.Filename,
                                    config.Debug);
            sender.Run();
        }
    }
  }
}
```

Before you can run the program, you have to change the name of the executable. Follow these steps to do so:

1. Right-click the Project file in the Solution Explorer.

2. Click Properties. This will open the Project Properties window.

3. Click the Application tab,

4. Change the Assembly Name to ncp.

5. Click the Save All icon.

Figure 4-5 shows the Project Properties window.

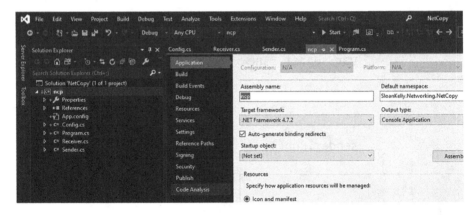

Figure 4-5. *The project properties window with ncp as the assembly name*

To try this program, you have to run it from the command line. Two command prompt windows are required—one for the server and the other for the client.

To receive a picture, on one command prompt window, the output might look like this after an image has been sent:

```
$ ncp troncopy2.jpg
Listening for connection
Size of file received is 2330429 byte(s)
```

On a client, the output might look like:

```
$ ncp -ip 127.0.0.1 -port 9021 tron.jpg
Sent 2330429 byte(s)
Finished!
```

The TcpListener and Socket classes makes things easier, but to make things really easy, the .Net framework also has another class called TcpClient. This class wraps the Socket class into a neat package. You'll look at how the TcpClient can be used to talk to a TcpListener next.

TcpClient Connections

The TcpClient class connects to a remote server and is used on the server to refer to a remote connection from another machine. The TcpClient class exposes a NetworkStream that is used to read and write data.

While it is certainly possible to use synchronous methods with TcpClient, this book will be avoiding them in favor of the asynchronous versions.

The TcpClient wraps the Socket class and contains an internal buffer. Because you're using the asynchronous methods, this buffer is returned when the read operation is completed.

Sockets vs. TcpClient and TcpListener

When should you choose to use sockets or the TcpClient/TcpListener classes very much depends on how the client and server will connect. If you are using TCP, then using TcpClient and TcpListener makes sense. They act as wrappers around the Socket class and use TCP over IPv4 or IPv6.

Sockets are not protocol specific. This is why when you create a socket you get a greater number of options for socket and protocol type. A socket can be UDP or TCP. See the Socket class' constructor for details.

Connecting to a Server Using TcpClient

To connect to a server running a connection-oriented TCP service, you should use the TcpClient class. The Connect() method connects to a server. The method takes either an endpoint or a separate IP address in the form of a string and a port number (an integer). The EndPoint class contains the IP address and the port number, combined. Listing 4-21 shows how a client could connect to a server running on the local machine on port 9021.

Listing 4-21. Connecting to a Service Running on Port 9021 on the Local Machine

```
var client = new TcpClient();
client.Connect("127.0.0.1", _port);
```

Sending Data Using TcpClient

Data is sent to the client using the client's network stream. It is possible to use a `BinaryReader` and `BinaryWriter` around the `NetworkStream` of the client, but it involves having two threads—one for the read and one for the write. It is easier to use the asynchronous method on the `NetworkStream` called `BeginWrite`, as shown in Listing 4-22.

Listing 4-22. Writing Data to a Remote Server Using the BeginWrite() Method of NetworkStream

```
var stream = client.GetStream();
var msg = Encoding.ASCII.GetBytes("Message to send");
client.GetStream()
      .BeginWrite(msg, 0, msg.Length, Send_Complete, client);
```

The `BeginWrite()` method takes five arguments:

- The byte array buffer containing the message to send
- The offset from the buffer
- The number of bytes to send
- The callback method
- The state. This can be anything, but it is recommended that at least the client be used as the state object

Listing 4-23 shows the contents of the Send_Complete method that will be called when the operation ends.

Listing 4-23. The callback Send_Complete Method Used to Complete the Transaction

```
void Send_Complete(IAsyncResult ar)
{
    if (ar.IsCompleted)
    {
        var client = ar.AsyncState as TcpClient;
        client.GetStream()
            .EndWrite(ar);
    }
}
```

The state object is contained in the AsyncState property of the IAsyncResult. Because you passed in the TcpClient, it can be used directly here to obtain the NetworkStream used to end the write transaction.

Reading Data Using a TcpClient

The TcpClient is used to represent a connection with a remote machine. This means that the TcpClient is used on the actual machine requesting the data (the client), as well as on the server as a reference to the connection with the client. Both the client and the server will use the TcpClient to receive messages.

Listing 4-24 shows how to receive a message using the NetworkStream's BeginRead() asynchronous method.

Listing 4-24. Asynchronous Reception of a Message Using a TcpClient

```
var state = new StateObject(client, buffer);
client.GetStream()
    .BeginRead(buffer,
               0,
               State.Buffer.Length,
               Client_Received,
               state);
```

The `BeginRead()` method takes five parameters:

- The buffer used to store the incoming message

- The offset inside the buffer where new messages will be received

- The number of bytes to receive

- The callback

- The state object

The state object `StateObject`, shown in Listing 4-25, contains the TcpClient and the buffer used to receive data. This is required because the callback will use both the TcpClient instance and the buffer. Because there can only be one state object, a new class needs to be constructed to hold the reference to the TcpClient and the receive buffer.

Listing 4-25. The StateObject Class

```
using System.Net.Sockets;

public class StateObject
{
    public TcpClient Client { get; }
```

```
    public NetworkStream Stream => Client.GetStream();

    public byte[] Buffer { get; }

    public ClientStateObject(TcpClient client,
                                int bufferSize = 1024)
    {
        Client = client;
        Buffer = new byte[bufferSize];
    }
}
```

Because the buffer is integral to the state, it is created in the constructor. Listing 4-26 shows the Client_Received callback where the StateObject is used.

Listing 4-26. The Client_Received Callback

```
private void Client_Received(IAsyncResult ar)
{
    if (ar.IsCompleted)
    {
        var state = ar.AsyncState as StateObject;
        var bytesIn = state.Stream.EndRead(ar);

        if (bytesIn > 0)
        {
            var msg = Encoding.ASCII
                            .GetString(state.Buffer,
                                        0,
                                        bytesIn);
            print($"From client: {msg}");
        }
```

```
        var newState = new StateObject(state.Client);
        state.Stream
            .BeginRead(state.Buffer,
                        0,
                        state.Buffer.Length,
                        Client_Received,
                        newState);
    }
}
```

The state object is read from the AsyncState property of the
IAsyncResult. The network stream read is completed by calling the
EndRead() method and this returns the number of bytes received.

Similar to the socket example earlier, this might not be the complete
message and you will have to listen for more. This is why there is a call to
BeginRead() at the very end of this method.

TcpListener: Accepting a TcpClient Connection

With the previous example using sockets, TcpListener also allows
incoming connections from a TcpClient. The BeginAcceptTcpClient()
method takes two parameters:

- A callback to be called when a connection is made

- A state object

It is recommended to use at least the TcpListener as the state object.
Listing 4-27 shows how a TcpListener would start accepting an inbound
TcpClient connection.

Listing 4-27. TcpListener Accepting an Asynchronous Inbound
TcpClient connection

```
var Listener = new TcpListener(IPAddress.Any, 9021);
listener.Start();
listener.BeginAcceptTcpClient(Socket_Connected, listener);
```

Listing 4-28 illustrates an example callback when a client is connected.
At the end of the method there is a further call to accept an incoming
connection. Without this, no other client could connect to your service.

Listing 4-28. Example Callback to Accept a TCP Client

```
private void Socket_Connected(IAsyncResult ar)
{
    if (ar.IsCompleted)
    {
        var listener = (ar.AsyncState as TcpListener);
        var client = listener.EndAcceptTcpClient(ar);
        // TO DO: Something with client

        listener.BeginAcceptTcpClient(Socket_Connected,
                                      listener);
    }
}
```

Note   If you want to accept more than one connection, you have to
re-call BeginAcceptTcpClient() when a client connects.

Don't worry about timing. Clients are buffered in a queue as
they connect and are presented to you one at a time. This is handled
automatically by the operating system too.

Hello World Example Using TcpClient and TcpListener

In this section, you see how to create a Hello World example using the TcpClient and TcpListener. You will revisit the Unity project from earlier in this chapter. Follow these steps:

1. Create a new scene in the project.

2. In the Scripts folder, create a new C# script file called TcpListenClientBehaviour.

3. In the Scripts folder, create a new C# script file called TcpClientAsyncBehaviour.

4. In the Scripts folder, create a new C# script file called ClientStateObject.

5. Drag and drop the TcpClientAsyncBehaviour script file onto the MainCamera in the scene.

6. Drag and drop the TcpListenClientBehaviour script file onto the MainCamera in the scene.

7. Save the scene as AsyncClients.

You should now have the project hierarchy shown in Figure 4-6.

Figure 4-6. *The project hierarchy after completing the steps to add the TcpClient script files*

With those steps complete, you will now fill in the script files that were just created. Listing 4-29 is the full script of the `ClientStateObject` class. This class is the state object used when receiving data from the client. It contains a reference to the `TcpClient` as well as the buffer that data is received into. Replace the current contents of the `ClientStateObject` script with Listing 4-29.

Listing 4-29. The ClientStateObject Script

```
using System.Net.Sockets;

public class ClientStateObject
{
    public TcpClient Client { get; }
    public NetworkStream Stream => Client.GetStream();
    public byte[] Buffer { get; }
```

```
    public ClientStateObject(TcpClient client,
                                int bufferSize = 1024)
    {
        Client = client;
        Buffer = new byte[bufferSize];
    }
}
```

Save the script file. The `TcpListenClientBehaviour` class will contain the `TcpListener`. It will be used to accept incoming client connections. By default, the server will run on any IP address on port 9021. This can be changed by altering the value of _port or in the Inspector in the Unity Editor.

Replace the contents of the `TcpListenClientBehaviour` script file with the code in Listing 4-30.

Listing 4-30. The TcpListenClientBehaviour Script

```
using System;
using System.Net;
using System.Net.Sockets;
using System.Text;
using UnityEngine;

public class TcpListenClientBehaviour : MonoBehaviour
{
    private TcpListener _listener;

    [HideInInspector]
    public bool _isReady;

    [Tooltip("The port the service is running on")]
    public int _port = 9021;
```

```
void Start()
{
    _listener = new TcpListener(IPAddress.Any,
                                    _port);
    _listener.Start();
    _listener.BeginAcceptTcpClient(Socket_Connected,
                                    _listener);
    _isReady = true;
}

private void OnDestroy()
{
    _listener?.Stop();
    _listener = null;
}
private void Socket_Connected(IAsyncResult ar)
{
    if (ar.IsCompleted)
    {
        var client = (ar.AsyncState as TcpListener)
                    .EndAcceptTcpClient(ar);
        var state = new ClientStateObject(client);

        client.GetStream()
            .BeginRead(state.Buffer,
                        0,
                        state.Buffer.Length,
                        Client_Received,
                        state);
    }
}
```

```
private void Client_Received(IAsyncResult ar)
{
    if (ar.IsCompleted)
    {
        var state = ar.AsyncState as ClientStateObject;
        var bytesIn = state.Stream.EndRead(ar);

        if (bytesIn > 0)
        {
            var msg = Encoding.ASCII
                            .GetString(state.Buffer,
                                        0,
                                        bytesIn);
            print($"From client: {msg}");
        }

        var newState = new ClientStateObject(state.Client);
        state.Stream
            .BeginRead(state.Buffer,
                        0,
                        state.Buffer.Length,
                        Client_Received,
                        newState);

    }
}
}
```

Save the file. Finally, Listing 4-31 contains the contents of
TcpClientAsyncBehaviour. Replace the current contents of the
TcpClientAsyncBehaviour script file with the code in Listing 4-31. The
assumption is that the client is connecting to a server running locally on
port 9031, but those values can be changed in the code or through the
Unity Editor's Inspector. Don't forget to save the file.

Listing 4-31. The TcpClientAsyncBehaviour Class

```
using System;
using System.Collections;
using System.Net.Sockets;
using System.Text;
using UnityEngine;

[RequireComponent(typeof(TcpListenClientBehaviour))]
public class TcpClientAsyncBehaviour : MonoBehaviour
{
    private TcpClient _client;

    [Tooltip("The server's IP address")]
    public string _ipAddress = "127.0.0.1";

    [Tooltip("The port the service is running on")]
    public int _port = 9021;

    IEnumerator Start()
    {
        var listener = GetComponent<TcpListenClientBehaviour>();
        while (!listener._isReady)
        {
            yield return null;
        }
        _client = new TcpClient();
        _client.Connect(_ipAddress, _port);
        var msg = Encoding.ASCII.GetBytes("Hello, from
        TcpClient!");
```

```
    _client.GetStream()
            .BeginWrite(msg,
                        0,
                        msg.Length,
                        Send_Complete,
                        _client);
}

private void Send_Complete(IAsyncResult ar)
{
    if (ar.IsCompleted)
    {
        var client = ar.AsyncState as TcpClient;
        client.GetStream()
                .EndWrite(ar);
    }
}
}
```

When you run the program in Unity, the console should, as shown in Figure 4-7, show the message received from the client.

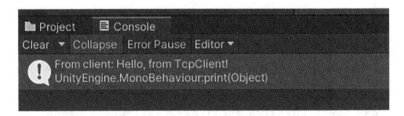

Figure 4-7. *The console output after running the scene containing the TcpClient example*

Tic-Tac-Toe

Tic-Tac-Toe—also known as Naughts and Crosses or Xs and Os—is a game played on a 3x3 grid. The goal is to be the first to place three tokens in a line on the grid. Each player takes turn placing their token—an X or an O on a blank grid square. The game is popular because the rules are simple and you only need a flat surface and something to draw the shapes on. Figure 4-8 shows a typical game in progress.

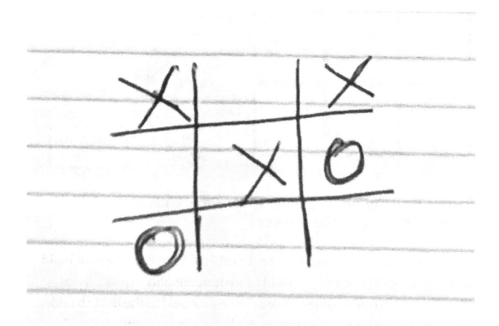

Figure 4-8. *An in-progress game of Tic-Tac-Toe played on a piece of paper. X is about to win*

Games can end in one of two ways; X or O can win by creating a row of tokens horizontally, vertically, or diagonally. The game can also end in a tie, sometimes referred to as a "cat's game." This is when there is no winner and no more moves are available, i.e., the board is full.

In the remaining pages of this chapter, you are going to create a client-server networked version of Tic-Tac-Toe that you can play with someone on their device. Figure 4-9 shows the same game as earlier, but in progress on the finished Tic-Tac-Toe client-server version you will build.

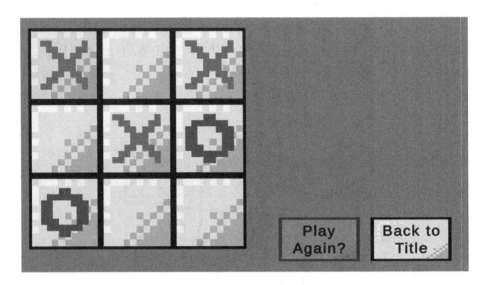

Figure 4-9. *An in-progress game of Tic-Tac-Toe played in the networked game. X is about to win*

This project will use the `TcpClient` and `TcpListener` classes to build the client-server application. To add more functionality, these classes will be wrapped inside some custom classes, located in the `NetLib` folder. These classes will help you maintain the list of clients connected to the server, messaging events and serialization/deserialization. You could just as easily not write these additional classes and code everything into the tic-tac-toe game itself. Abstraction of the network layer provides a better way to separate the game from the networking classes.

To pass data between the client and the server, you will use a simple serialization protocol. The messages passed will be simple text messages. The first line will contain a header with the size of the payload.

The payload is the actual message being sent. The payload contains the state of the board and the current player as well as a command to inform the client application what state to be in.

The client and server will use a small finite state machine (FSM) to control the current state of the program. See https://en.wikipedia.org/wiki/Finite-state_machine for more details on finite state machines.

The Tic-Tac-Toe game will allow one player to act as a server and allow another to connect. The player running the server will also connect via the network, but this will be transparent to the player.

When the game starts, the players are shown the title page, as shown in Figure 4-10. It contains two options—start or join a server.

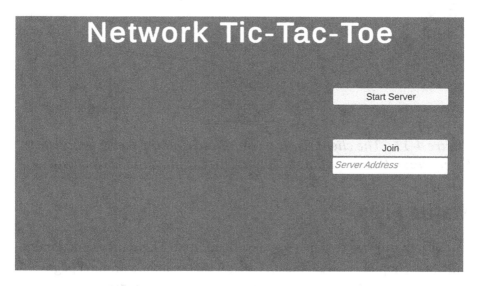

Figure 4-10. *The title screen showing the Start Server, Join, and IP address controls*

When the server starts, a client is automatically created and joins the server. The first client to join is always X. The second client will be another player running on another device. When the second client joins, the game starts and X gets to make their first turn. Then O, and so on, until the game ends. It isn't possible to click a square when another player is choosing their grid square.

Each cell or button click on the client sends a message to the server. This will result in a message being sent back to all the clients.

Clients can only send commands to the server and the server can only send updates to the command. The cycle is shown in Figure 4-11 with one client, but in the actual application, the updates will be sent to both clients.

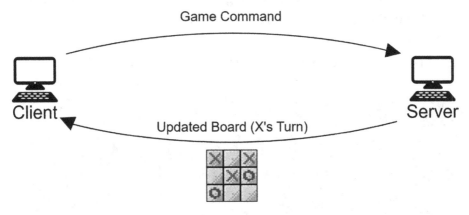

Figure 4-11. *The client sends a command and the server broadcasts the updated board, game state, and current player to each client*

Starter Files

A project of this size requires some work up front. The source code for this and other chapters is available on GitHub via the book's product page, located at https://www.apress.com/us/book/9781484273579.

Getting Started

The project uses the Canvas and UI controls to build the game and its various states. To create the starter project, follow these steps:

1. Create a new 2D project in Unity called `Tic-Tac-Toe`.

2. Download the `tictactoe-starter.unitypackage`
    file from the book's GitHub repo.

3. Double-click the package to install it into the open
    project.

You should now have a scene called `StartHere` and the list of assets, as
shown in Figure 4-12.

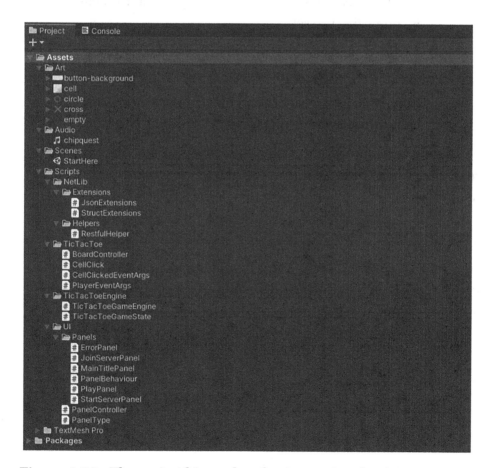

Figure 4-12. *The project hierarchy after importing the tictactoe-
starter.unitypackage*

143

The Game Architecture

The game uses the Canvas/UI MonoBehaviours provided by Unity to create a series of panels that are nested under the TicTacToeUI game object:

- Title – A panel with the Start Server and Join buttons

- WaitForOpponent – A panel that is displayed when the server is waiting for an opponent to join

- WaitForServer – A panel that is displayed when a client is connecting to a server

- Error – A panel used to display an error message like "server not found" to the player

- Play – The panel that displays the tic-tac-toe board and allows the players to interact with each other

What is currently missing are the networking portions of the game, something you'll need! You also need some way to glue the UI to the networking.

The Client

The tic-tac-toe game has been built using the client-server model. Figure 4-13 shows some of the classes used on the client side of the game and how they communicate internally and with the server.

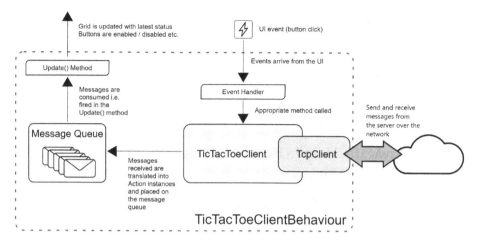

Figure 4-13. *The TicTacToeClientBehaviour class and how it communicates internally with the UI and to and from the server via the TcpClient*

The TicTacToeClientBehaviour provides the glue code between the UI—the play grid and the buttons—and the network communications.

Even though the client handles events, it does not directly respond to them and instead waits for confirmation of the action from the server. This ensures the integrity of the game state.

Each time the player clicks a button in the UI, it is translated into an event. The event handler on TicTacToeClientBehaviour calls a method on the TicTacToeClient, which in turn sends a message to the server. When messages are received from the server, they are placed on a queue and processed one at a time in the Update() method of the TicTacToeClientBehaviour. These messages update the visual state of the game and the circle is complete.

Note   You should never trust the client! Confirm all actions on the server to ensure that the game is being played fairly.

145

The Client Events

The TicTacToeClientBehaviour subscribes to three events exposed by the BoardController class:

- CellClicked – Fired when the player clicks a cell in the tic-tac-toe grid

- PlayAgainClicked – Fired when the player clicks the Play Again button

- ReturnToTitleClick – Fired when the player clicks the Return to Title button

In each case, the handlers call methods on the TicTacToeClient that will send a message to the server. No UI update is performed in these event handlers.

To connect to the server, a new game object will be created and the TicTacToeClientBehaviour component will be attached to it.

Note   The entire application will use standard .Net events to decouple the classes. These will be used on the networking side to inform subscribers when a message has been received.

The TicTacToeClient

The TicTacToeClient provides several services for the TicTacToeClientBehaviour:

- Handles sending messages to the server. Methods are exposed to TicTacToeClientBehaviour to send those messages without it having to explicitly know how to format them.

- Handles incoming messages from the server.

- Provides event handlers that the
  TicTacToeClientBehaviour can subscribe to for
  starting the game, toggling the active player, showing
  the winner screen, and quitting to return to the title.

The TicTacToeClient contains an instance of the NetworkClient
class. This will provide the underlying network access.

NetworkClient

The NetworkClient class wraps the .Net TcpClient class and a buffer into
a single class. This makes the reception and transmission of data to and
from a client easier. Internally, there is a MessageBuffer class that will be
used to store large messages received from the server. Once a complete
message has been received, anyone subscribing to the MessageReceived
event will be notified.

It should be noted that any messages received will be on a thread that
is not the main thread. There must be a way to send the message from the
remote machine to the main thread. In the game, this will be implemented
using a very simple message queue.

The Message Queue

The central part of the TicTacToeClientBehaviour is the message queue.
Messages received using the asynchronous method of BeginRead() of the
TcpClient are not received on the main thread. In order to get them onto
the main thread, we will employ a simple message queue that uses actions.
Listing 4-32 shows the implementation of a simple message queue using
the Queue<T> class and demonstrates placing items on the queue and
taking them off and executing them one at a time.

Listing 4-32. Implementing a Simple Message Queue

```
var _actions = new Queue<Action>();
// Put an action on the queue
Action action = () => print("Hello there!");
lock (_actions)
{
    _actions.Enqueue(action);
}

// Cycle through the actions on the queue,
// executing one at a time
lock(_actions)
{
    while (_actions.Count > 0)
    {
        _actions.Dequeue().Invoke();
    }
}
```

Each time there is an interaction with the queue, you must lock it. This prevents other threads from accessing the message queue while an action is enqueued/dequeued.

Note   Use the lock() pattern to ensure that other threads cannot access the data at the same time.

The Server

TicTacToeServer is based on the NetworkServer<T> class that contains a TcpListener instance. The TicTacToeServer class handles the network traffic and the TicTacToeGameServer class acts as a bridge between the network traffic (in and out bound) and the game logic. Figure 4-14 shows how the server classes pass messages internally and externally to the connected clients.

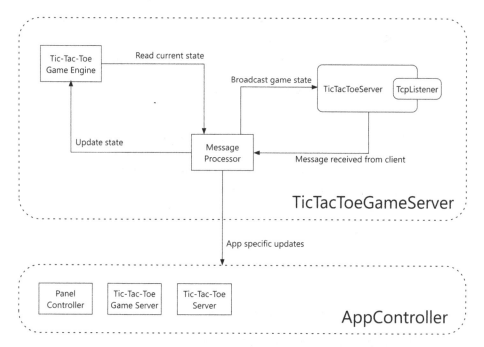

Figure 4-14. *The relationship between the classes used in the server part of the game*

The `AppController` class extends `MonoBehaviour` and has links to the `PanelController`; it handles the user interaction with the title screen, which includes event handlers for the Join and Start Server buttons.

The `NetworkServer<T>` class contains a `TcpListener` instance and maintains a list of clients using the `NetworkClientCollection` class. Each time a client connects, an event is fired. The class can also limit the maximum number of clients that can connect. You will be using this feature in this application because only two people can play tic-tac-toe. The class is generic because, when a message is received, it is deserialized into the correct class/struct instance.

Serialization

To minimize the errors in serialization/deserialization, a factory class called GameSerialization will be created. This will contain functions to generate the messages in the correct format. It will also provide a way to deserialize a byte array into a message.

The message class is GameMessage and contains three fields:

- messageType – An enumeration that represents the type of message being passed

- playerId (int) – The currently active player

- boardState (int[]) – An array of integer values that represents the current state of the board. This means that there will always be nine values in this array; one for each grid square

The boardState will contain one of three possible values for each grid square:

- 0 – The grid square is unoccupied

- 1 – An X is placed in the grid square

- 2 – An O is placed in the grid square

Messages passed from server to client will always contain the current state of the game.

Messages passed from client to server will provide the server with the player ID (which could be validated on the server side); the boardState value contains an array with a single integer representing the move if the messageType is MessageType.ClientMakeMove. All other messages from the client to the server will have an array with a single 0 (zero) in them, because those commands do not need extra information.

The payload format uses a simple colon-separated list in this format:

`messageType:playerId:gridState`

Where `messageType` is the type of message being transmitted, `playerId` is the ID of the player (1 – first player, 2 – second player) who has control of the board, and the `gridState` is a comma-separated list of values representing the state of the board. For example, the following message will let the client know whose turn it is while indicating the state of the board. The top left of the board is occupied with an X (player 1):

```
Size: 38
ServerTogglePlayer:2:1,0,0,0,0,0,0,0,0
```

Notice that the entire message includes the header. The header will be stripped out and the payload will be read separately by the deserializer.

NetLib Classes

To abstract the networking code from the main logic of the Tic-Tac-Toe game, you will create some wrapper classes around `TcpClient` and `TcpListener`. These classes will provide you with ways to handle passing messages across the network as well as maintain client connections. Follow these instructions to create the script files for the new NetLib classes:

1. Create a new C# script file in the `Scripts/NetLib` folder called `MessageBuffer`.

2. Create a new C# script file in the `Scripts/NetLib` folder called `NetworkClient`.

3. Create a new C# script file in the `Scripts/NetLib` folder called `NetworkClientConnection`.

4. Create a new C# script file in the `Scripts/NetLib` folder called `NetworkServer`.

5. Create a new folder called `Events` inside the `NetLib` folder.

6. Create a new C# script file in the `Scripts/NetLib/Events` folder called `MessageReceivedEventArgs`.

7. Create a new C# script file in the `Scripts/NetLib/Events` folder called `NetworkClientEventArgs`.

8. Create a new C# script file in the `Scripts/NetLib/Events` folder called `PayloadEventArgs`.

With all those files created, you should have a hierarchy inside your `NetLib` folder that looks like Figure 4-15.

Figure 4-15. *The NetLib script hierarchy after completing the tasks*

With all those files created, it's time to start adding the code. The classes have been separated into logical breaks to give a little insight to their purpose and how they can be used outside of this project.

MessageBuffer Class

The MessageBuffer class is located in the NetLib folder. It is used to store incoming large messages from a remote device. On completion, the IsComplete property is set. Listing 4-33 shows the contents of the MessageBuffer class. Open the MessageBuffer.cs file and replace the contents with the code in Listing 4-33.

Listing 4-33. The MessageBuffer Class

```csharp
using System;

public class MessageBuffer
{
    private int _currentOffset;
    public byte[] Buffer { get; }

    public bool IsComplete => _currentOffset == Buffer.Length;

    public int Length => Buffer.Length;

    public MessageBuffer(int size)
    {
        Buffer = new byte[size];
    }

    public void Append(byte[] source, int length = -1)
    {
        var len = length > 0 ? length : source.Length;
        Array.Copy(source, 0, Buffer, _currentOffset, len);
        _currentOffset += len;
    }
}
```

When a message has been received, subscribers should be notified. The MessageReceivedEventArgs will be used with an event handler to provide subscribers with the needed information. Listing 4-34 contains the contents of the MessageReceivedEventArgs class. Open the NetLib/Events/MessageReceivedEventArgs script file and replace the contents with the code in Listing 4-34.

Listing 4-34. The MessageReceivedEventArgs Class

```
using System;

public class MessageReceivedEventArgs : EventArgs
{
    public byte[] Data { get; }

    public MessageReceivedEventArgs(byte[] data, int length)
    {
        Data = new byte[length];
        Array.Copy(data, Data, length);
    }
}
```

NetworkClient Class

The NetworkClient class is used by the client (unsurprisingly!) and the server to allow for two-way communication between the client and server. It contains an instance of TcpClient to provide the networking and a MessageBuffer to hold larger messages.

It is based on a simple text-based protocol that has a header describing the size of the payload and the payload itself. The header and payload are separated by a single \n (newline) character.

The format of the header is as follows:

```
Size: size-of-header
```

Where size-of-header is an integer that is the length of the payload in bytes. It is assumed that the messages passed in are in the correct format. For simplicity, there is no error checking, which can be added later.

When a message has been received in full, the MessageReceived event is triggered. This uses the MessageReceivedEventArgs class that you created earlier.

Listing 4-35 contains the full listing for NetworkClient. Open the NetworkClient script file in the NetLib folder and replace it with the following listing.

Listing 4-35. The NetworkClient Class

```
using System;
using System.Net.Sockets;
using System.Text;
using System.Text.RegularExpressions;

public class NetworkClient
{
    public const int DefaultBufferSize = 4096;

    private readonly byte[] _buffer;
    private TcpClient _client;

    private MessageBuffer _store;

    private bool ClientCanRead
    {
        get
        {
            return _client != null &&
                    _client.Connected &&
                    _client.GetStream().CanRead;
        }
    }
```

```
private bool ClientCanWrite
{
    get
    {
        return _client != null &&
                _client.Connected &&
                _client.GetStream().CanWrite;
    }
}

public event EventHandler<MessageReceivedEventArgs>
MessageReceived;

public NetworkClient(TcpClient client,
                    int bufferSize = DefaultBufferSize)
{
    _client = client;
    _buffer = new byte[bufferSize];
    _client.GetStream().BeginRead(_buffer,
                                0,
                                _buffer.Length,
                                Remote_ReceivedMessage,
                                null);
}

public NetworkClient(int bufferSize = DefaultBufferSize)
{
    _buffer = new byte[bufferSize];
    _client = new TcpClient(AddressFamily.InterNetwork);
```

```
_client.GetStream().BeginRead(_buffer,
                              0,
                              _buffer.Length,
                              Remote_ReceivedMessage,
                              null);
}

public void Close()
{
    _client.Close();
    _client.Dispose();
    _client = null;
}

public void Send(byte[] message)
{
    if (!ClientCanWrite)
    {
        return;
    }

    var header = $"Size: {message.Length}\n";
    var headerBytes = Encoding.ASCII.GetBytes(header);
    var fullMessage = new byte[message.Length + header.
    Length];

    Array.Copy(headerBytes, fullMessage, headerBytes.
    Length);
    Array.Copy(message, 0, fullMessage, headerBytes.Length,
    message.Length);
```

```
        _client.GetStream().BeginWrite(fullMessage,
                                        0,
                                        fullMessage.Length,
                                        Write_Callback,
                                        null);
    }

    private void Remote_ReceivedMessage(IAsyncResult ar)
    {
        if (ar.IsCompleted && ClientCanRead)
        {
            var bytesReceived = _client.GetStream()
                                        .EndRead(ar);
            if (bytesReceived > 0)
            {
                if (_store != null)
                {
                    AppendToStore(bytesReceived);
                }
                else
                {
                    ReadBuffer(bytesReceived);
                }
                Array.Clear(_buffer, 0, _buffer.Length);
                _client.GetStream()
                        .BeginRead(_buffer,
                                    0,
                                    _buffer.Length,
                                    Remote_ReceivedMessage,
                                    null);
            }
        }
    }
}
```

```
private void ReadBuffer(int bytesReceived)
{
    var text = Encoding.ASCII
                        .GetString(_buffer,
                                   0,
                                   bytesReceived);
    var sizeMatch = new Regex("^[S|s]ize:\\s");
    var match = sizeMatch.Match(text);
    if (match.Success)
    {
        var startOfLength = match.Index + match.Length;
        var endOfLine = text.IndexOf('\n', startOfLength);
        var lengthStr = text.Substring(startOfLength,
                            endOfLine - startOfLength);
        var length = int.Parse(lengthStr);
        var payloadSoFar = text.Substring(endOfLine + 1,
                                    text.Length -
                                    (endOfLine + 1));

        var payload = Encoding.ASCII
                            .GetBytes(payloadSoFar);
        if (payloadSoFar.Length == length)
        {
            var args = new
                    MessageReceivedEventArgs(payload,
                                        payload.Length);
            MessageReceived?.Invoke(this, args);
        }
}
```

```
            else
            {
                _store = new MessageBuffer(length);
                _store.Append(payload);
            }
        }
    }

    private void AppendToStore(int bytesReceived)
    {
        _store.Append(_buffer, bytesReceived);
        if (_store.IsComplete)
        {
            var args = new MessageReceivedEventArgs(_store.
            Buffer, _store.Length);
            MessageReceived?.Invoke(this, args);
            _store = null;
        }
    }

    private void Write_Callback(IAsyncResult ar)
    {
        if (ar.IsCompleted)
        {
            _client.GetStream().EndWrite(ar);
        }
    }
}
```

Note   Don't forget to save the files as you type!

On the server, the clients are stored inside a `NetworkClientCollection` class. This class keeps the clients together and provides a single `MessageReceived` event handler that subscribers can hook into. The subscribers also receive the `NetworkClient` instance that sent the message.

Open `NetworkClientCollection` in the `NetLib` folder and replace it with the code in Listing 4-36.

Listing 4-36. The NetworkClientCollection Class

```csharp
using System;
using System.Collections;
using System.Collections.Generic;

public class NetworkClientCollection :
IEnumerable<NetworkClient>
{
    private readonly List<NetworkClient> _clients =
                            new List<NetworkClient>();

    public int Count => _clients.Count;

    public event EventHandler<MessageReceivedEventArgs>
                                    MessageReceived;

    public void Add(NetworkClient client)
    {
        _clients.Add(client);
        client.MessageReceived += Client_MessageReceived;
    }

    public IEnumerator<NetworkClient> GetEnumerator()
    {
        return _clients.GetEnumerator();
    }
```

```csharp
public void DisconnectAll()
{
    foreach (var client in _clients)
    {
        client.Close();
    }

    _clients.Clear();
}

private void Client_MessageReceived(object sender,
                              MessageReceivedEventArgs e)
{
    MessageReceived?.Invoke(sender, e);
}

IEnumerator IEnumerable.GetEnumerator()
{
    return GetEnumerator();
}
}
```

NetworkServer

The NetworkServer class is located in the NetLib folder; it handles the incoming connections and maintains a list of connected clients. The maximum number of clients allowed to connect can be set at runtime. The NetworkServer is a wrapper around the TcpListener class. It provides four events for subscribers:

- ClientConnected – Subscribers are informed each time a client connects.

- ConnectionOverflow – Subscribers are informed when a client tries to connect but the maximum number of connections has been exceeded.

- PayloadReceived – Subscribers are informed when a payload has been received from one of the clients.

- ClientListFull – Subscribers are informed when the maximum number of clients have connected. This fires when the current client connects and the number of connected clients equals the maximum allowed.

The NetworkServer class is an abstract class. Each game needs to provide its own subclass and implement a single method, CreatePayload(). Optionally, subclasses can override the OnClientConnected() method.

Before you create the NetworkServer class, you need to create the two remaining event argument classes—NetworkClientEventArgs and PayloadEventArgs.

Open the NetworkClientEventArgs script file in NetLib/Events folder. Replace the existing code with the contents in Listing 4-37. Save the file.

Listing 4-37. The NetworkClientEventArgs Class

```
using System;

public class NetworkClientEventArgs : EventArgs
{
    public NetworkClient { get; }

    public NetworkClientEventArgs(NetworkClient networkClient)
    {
        NetworkClient = networkClient;
    }
}
```

Now open the PayloadEventArgs script file in the NetLib/Events folder. Replace the existing code with the contents of Listing 4-38. Save the file.

Listing 4-38. The PayloadEventArgs Class

```
public class PayloadEventArgs<T>
{
    public T Payload { get; }

    public PayloadEventArgs(T payload)
    {
        Payload = payload;
    }
}
```

With those two classes complete, you can now finish the NetworkServer class. It is a generic class that takes a type that represents the payload. For this game, that will be the GameMessage class. As you will see later, the TicTacToeServer extends NetworkServer and provides this generic parameter.

Open the NetworkServer script file located in the NetLib folder. Replace the contents of this file with the code in Listing 4-39 and save the file.

Listing 4-39. The NetworkServer Abstract Class

```
using System;
using System.Net;
using System.Net.Sockets;

public abstract class NetworkServer<T>
{
    private readonly NetworkClientCollection _clients =
                            new NetworkClientCollection();
    private readonly TcpListener _listener;
    private readonly int _maxConnections;
```

```
public event EventHandler<NetworkClientEventArgs>
ClientConnected;
public event EventHandler<NetworkClientEventArgs>
ConnectionOverflow;
public event EventHandler<PayloadEventArgs<T>>
PayloadReceived;
public event EventHandler ClientListFull;

public NetworkServer(int port, int maxConnections = 16)
{
    _listener = new TcpListener(IPAddress.Any, port);
    _maxConnections = maxConnections;
    _clients.MessageReceived += Client_MessageReceived;
}

public void Start()
{
    _listener.Start();
    _listener.BeginAcceptTcpClient(Listener_
    ClientConnected, null);
}

public void Stop()
{
    _clients.DisconnectAll();
    _listener.Stop();
}

private void Listener_ClientConnected(IAsyncResult ar)
{
    if (ar.IsCompleted)
    {
        var client = _listener.EndAcceptTcpClient(ar);
        var networkClient = new NetworkClient(client);
```

```
            if (_clients.Count == _maxConnections)
            {
                ConnectionOverflow?.Invoke(this,
                    new NetworkClientEventArgs(networkClient));
            }
            else
            {
                _clients.Add(networkClient);
                OnClientConnected(networkClient);

                if (_clients.Count == _maxConnections)
                {
                    ClientListFull?.Invoke(this,
                                        EventArgs.Empty);
                }
                else
                {
                    _listener.BeginAcceptTcpClient(Listener_
                    ClientConnected, null);
                }
            }
        }
    }

    private void Client_MessageReceived(object sender,
                            MessageReceivedEventArgs e)
    {
        var payload = CreatePayload(e.Data);
        PayloadReceived?.Invoke(sender,
                    new PayloadEventArgs<T>(payload));
    }
```

```
protected abstract T CreatePayload(byte[] message);

protected void Broadcast(byte[] message)
{
    foreach (var c in _clients)
    {
        c.Send(message);
    }
}

protected virtual void OnClientConnected(NetworkClient
                                          networkClient)
{
    ClientConnected?.Invoke(this,
            new NetworkClientEventArgs(networkClient));
}
}
```

Client and Server Classes

The classes you just added to NetLib are generic enough that you can use
them pretty much in any project you want. They provide a lightweight
TCP-based protocol (small header and payload) that is easy to use. But in
order to get the functionality that you require for this game, you have to
build game-specific classes that sit on top.

Follow these instructions to build the classes that you will need. Once
the script files have been created, you can get started populating them.

1. Create a new folder in the Scripts folder called
   TicTacToeNetworking.

2. Create a new folder in Scripts/
   TicTacToeNetworking called Events.

3. Create a new C# script file called `GameMessageEventArgs` in `Scripts/TicTacToeNetworking/Events`.

4. Create a new C# script file in `Scripts/TicTacToeNetworking` called `GameMessage`.

5. Create a new C# script file in `Scripts/TicTacToeNetworking` called `GameSerialization`.

6. Create a new C# script file in `Scripts/TicTacToeNetworking` called `MessageType`.

7. Create a new C# script file in `Scripts/TicTacToeNetworking` called `TicTacToeClient`.

8. Create a new C# script file in `Scripts/TicTacToeNetworking` called `TicTacToeClientBehaviour`.

9. Create a new C# script file in `Scripts/TicTacToeNetworking` called `TicTacToeGameServer`.

10. Create a new C# script file in `Scripts/TicTacToeNetworking` called `TicTacToeServer`.

11. Create a new C# script file in `Scripts/UI` called `AppController`.

Messages

The game messages are sent between the classes using standard .Net event handlers. Each `GameMessage` consists of three elements:

- The message type, which is an enum value from `MessageType`

- The player ID

- The state of the tic-tac-toe grid as an array of integers

Open the MessageType script file. Replace the contents of this file with Listing 4-40 and save the file.

Listing 4-40. The MessageType Enumeration

```
public enum MessageType
{
    ServerStartGame,
    ServerTogglePlayer,
    ServerShowPodium,
    ClientMakeMove,
    ClientPlayAgain,
    ClientQuit
}
```

Open the GameMessage script file. Replace the contents of the GameMessage script file with Listing 4-41 and save the file.

Listing 4-41. GameMessage Struct

```
public struct GameMessage
{
    public MessageType;
    public int playerId;
    public int[] boardState;
}
```

The GameMessage instances are passed around using an EventHandler that emits a GameMessageEventArgs instance. Open the GameMessageEventArgs script file. Replace the contents of the file with Listing 4-42.

Listing 4-42. GameMessageEventArgs

```
using System;

public class GameMessageEventArgs : EventArgs
{
    public GameMessage Message { get; }

    public GameMessageEventArgs(GameMessage message)
    {
        Message = message;
    }
}
```

To make it easier to serialize game messages to a byte array and from a byte array to a GameMessage instance, a factory class called GameSerialization needs to be created. Open the GameSerialization script file and replace the contents of that file with Listing 4-43. Don't forget to save what you have done so far.

Listing 4-43. The GameSerialization Factory Class Helps Serialize and Deserialize GameMessage Instances

```
using System;
using System.Linq;
using System.Text;

public static class GameSerialization
{
    public static byte[] CreateMove(int playerId,
                                    int cellIndex)
    {
        return CreateMessage(playerId,
                             MessageType.ClientMakeMove,
                             new int[1] { cellIndex });
    }
```

```
public static byte[] CreatePlayAgain()
{
    return CreateMessage(0, MessageType.ClientPlayAgain);
}

public static byte[] CreateClientQuit()
{
    return CreateMessage(0, MessageType.ClientQuit);
}

public static byte[] CreatePodium(int currentPlayer,
                                  int[] boardState)
{
    return CreateMessage(currentPlayer,
                         MessageType.ServerShowPodium,
                         boardState);
}

public static byte[] CreateMessage(int playerId,
                                   MessageType type,
                                   int[] boardState = null)
{
    var state = boardState == null ||
                boardState.Length == 0 ? new int[1] { 0 }
                                       : boardState;
    var message = new GameMessage
    {
        boardState = state,
        messageType = type,
        playerId = playerId
    };

    return ToBytes(message);
}
```

```
    public static GameMessage FromBytes(byte[] message)
    {
        var str = Encoding.ASCII.GetString(message);
        var split = str.Split(":".ToCharArray());
        var messageType = (MessageType)Enum.
        Parse(typeof(MessageType),
                       split[0]);
        var playerId = int.Parse(split[1]);
        var payload = split[2].Split(',').Select(int.Parse);

        return new GameMessage
        {
            boardState = payload.ToArray(),
            messageType = messageType,
            playerId = playerId
        };
    }

    public static byte[] ToBytes(GameMessage message)
    {
        var str = $"{message.messageType}:{message.
playerId}:{string.Join(",", message.boardState)}";
        return Encoding.ASCII.GetBytes(str);
    }
}
```

Client Classes

There are two client classes used by the game—TicTacToeClient and
TicTacToClientBehaviour.

TicTacToeClient is a wrapper around NetworkClient and exposes a
number of events that subscribers can hook into. These events are fired
when a message is received from the server:

- StartGame – The server has indicated that the game is starting

- TogglePlayer – The active player has changed

- ShowPodium – Show the winners podium

- ReturnToTitle – The game should return to the title screen

The TicTacToeClientBehaviour is created when the player that is hosting the game starts the server or when a remote player joins a server. It uses the methods on the TicTacToeClient to send messages to the server.

Open the TicTacToeClient script file and replace the contents with the code shown in Listing 4-44.

Listing 4-44. The TicTacToeClient Script File

```
using System;

public class TicTacToeClient
{
    private readonly NetworkClient _client;

    public event EventHandler<GameMessageEventArgs> StartGame;
    public event EventHandler<GameMessageEventArgs> TogglePlayer;
    public event EventHandler<GameMessageEventArgs> ShowPodium;
    public event EventHandler ReturnToTitle;

    public TicTacToeClient(NetworkClient client)
    {
        _client = client;
        _client.MessageReceived += MessageReceived;
    }
}
```

```
public void PlayAgain()
{
    _client.Send(GameSerialization.CreatePlayAgain());
}

public void ReturnToLobby()
{
    _client.Send(GameSerialization.CreateClientQuit());
}

public void MakeMove(int index)
{
    _client.Send(GameSerialization.CreateMove(0, index));
}

public void Cleanup()
{
    _client.MessageReceived -= MessageReceived;
}

private void MessageReceived(object sender,
MessageReceivedEventArgs e)
{
    var data = new byte[e.Data.Length];
    Array.Copy(e.Data, data, e.Data.Length);

    var message = GameSerialization.FromBytes(data);
    switch (message.messageType)
    {
        case MessageType.ServerStartGame:
            StartGame?.Invoke(this, new GameMessageEvent
            Args(message));
            break;
```

```
            case MessageType.ServerTogglePlayer:
                TogglePlayer?.Invoke(this, new GameMessageEvent
                Args(message));
                break;
            case MessageType.ServerShowPodium:
                ShowPodium?.Invoke(this, new GameMessageEvent
                Args(message));
                break;
            case MessageType.ClientQuit:
                ReturnToTitle?.Invoke(this, EventArgs.Empty);
                break;
        }
    }
}
```

Open the TicTacToeClientBehaviour script file and replace the
contents with the code shown in Listing 4-45. This class will be instantiated
in the AppController class.

Listing 4-45. TicTacToeClientBehaviour Class

```
using System;
using System.Collections.Generic;
using System.Net.Sockets;
using UnityEngine;

public class TicTacToeClientBehaviour : MonoBehaviour
{
    private int _playerID;

    private NetworkClient _networkClient;
    private TicTacToeClient _client;
```

```csharp
    public AppController _app;
    public BoardController _board;

    private Queue<Action> _actions;

    void Awake()
    {
        _actions = new Queue<Action>();
    }

    void Update()
    {
        lock(_actions)
        {
            while (_actions.Count > 0)
            {
                _actions.Dequeue().Invoke();
            }
        }
    }

    private void OnDestroy()
    {
        lock (_actions)
        {
            _actions.Clear();
        }

        _client.ShowPodium -= Client_ShowPodium;
        _client.StartGame -= Client_StartGame;
        _client.TogglePlayer -= Client_TogglePlayer;
        _client.ReturnToTitle -= Client_ReturnToTitle;

        _board.CellClicked -= BoardCell_Clicked;
```

```
    _board.PlayAgainClicked -= PlayAgain_Clicked;
    _board.ReturnToTitleClicked -= ReturnToTitle_Clicked;

    _client.Cleanup();
}

public void Connect(TcpClient tcpClient)
{
    _networkClient = new NetworkClient(tcpClient);
    _client = new TicTacToeClient(_networkClient);
    _client.ShowPodium += Client_ShowPodium;
    _client.StartGame += Client_StartGame;
    _client.TogglePlayer += Client_TogglePlayer;
    _client.ReturnToTitle += Client_ReturnToTitle;

    _board.CellClicked += BoardCell_Clicked;
    _board.PlayAgainClicked += PlayAgain_Clicked;
    _board.ReturnToTitleClicked += ReturnToTitle_Clicked;
}

private void Client_ReturnToTitle(object sender, EventArgs e)
{
    Action action = () => _app.StopServer();
    lock (_actions)
    {
        _actions.Enqueue(action);
    }
}

private void ReturnToTitle_Clicked(object sender,
EventArgs e)
{
    _client.ReturnToLobby();
}
```

```csharp
private void PlayAgain_Clicked(object sender, EventArgs e)
{
    _client.PlayAgain();
}

private void BoardCell_Clicked(object sender,
CellClickedEventArgs e)
{
    _client.MakeMove(e.CellIndex);
}

private void Client_TogglePlayer(object sender,
GameMessageEventArgs e)
{
    lock (_actions)
    {
        _actions.Enqueue(() =>
        {
            _board.ToggleCellButtons(_playerID ==
            e.Message.playerId);
            _board.UpdateBoard(e.Message.boardState);
        });
    }
}

private void Client_StartGame(object sender,
GameMessageEventArgs e)
{
    Action action = () =>
    {
        _playerID = e.Message.playerId < 0 ? 2 : e.Message.
        playerId;
        _board.ResetBoard(e.Message.boardState);
```

```
        _board.ToggleCellButtons(_playerID == 1);
        _app._panels.ShowPanel(PanelType.Play);
    };

    lock (_actions)
    {
        _actions.Enqueue(action);
    }
}

private void Client_ShowPodium(object sender,
GameMessageEventArgs e)
{
    Action action = () =>
    {
        _board.UpdateBoard(e.Message.boardState);
        _board.ToggleCellButtons(false);
        _board.ToggleActionButtons(true);
        _board.BoardWinner(e.Message.playerId);
    };

    lock (_actions)
    {
        _actions.Enqueue(action);
    }
}
}
```

Note   Because `TicTacToeClientBehaviour` provides the link between the network messages and UI, a message queue has to be used to process the messages on the main thread.

Server Classes

There are two server classes—TicTacToeServer is the networking
component and TicTacToeGameServer is the part that interfaces
the networking code with the tic-tac-toe game engine. The
TicTacToeGameEngine class does not need to know that it is running a
networked game of tic-tac-toe. The TicTacToeGameServer provides some
code to bridge the actions coming from the client and the game.

The TicTacToeServer extends NetworkServer and provides it with
the generic argument—GameMessage, which is the struct you declared
earlier. Open the TicTacToeServer script file and replace it with the code
in Listing 4-46.

Listing 4-46. TicTacToeServer Class

```
using System.Collections.Generic;

public class TicTacToeServer : NetworkServer<GameMessage>
{
    private readonly List<NetworkClient> _players = new
    List<NetworkClient>();

    public TicTacToeServer(int port)
        : base(port, 2)
    {

    }

    public void StartGame()
    {
        SetCurrentPlayer(1, new int[9], MessageType.
        ServerStartGame);
    }
```

```csharp
public void QuitToTitle()
{
    _players.ForEach((p) => p.Send(GameSerialization.
    CreateClientQuit()));
}

public void SetCurrentPlayer(int currentPlayer,
int[] boardState, MessageType type = MessageType.
ServerTogglePlayer)
{
    for (int i = 0; i < _players.Count; i++)
    {
        var player = (i + 1 == currentPlayer) ?
        currentPlayer : -1;
        var message = GameSerialization
                        .CreateMessage(player, type,
                        boardState);

        _players[i].Send(message);
    }
}

public bool IsCurrentPlayer(NetworkClient client, int
currentPlayer)
{
    return (_players.IndexOf(client) + 1) == currentPlayer;
}

public void ShowPodium(int currentPlayer, int[] cells)
{
    Broadcast(GameSerialization.CreatePodium(currentPlayer,
    cells));
}
```

```
protected override GameMessage CreatePayload(byte[] message)
{
    return GameSerialization.FromBytes(message);
}

protected override void OnClientConnected(NetworkClient
networkClient)
{
    base.OnClientConnected(networkClient);
    _players.Add(networkClient);
}
}
```

As you have noticed, these are methods that wrap around network calls. The TicTacToeGameServer uses these methods to interact with the clients. Open the TicTacToeGameServer script file and replace the contents with Listing 4-47. Save the file.

Listing 4-47. TicTacToeGameServer Class

```
using System;

public class TicTacToeGameServer
{
    private readonly TicTacToeServer _server;
    private readonly TicTacToeGameEngine _engine;

    public TicTacToeGameServer(TicTacToeServer server)
    {
        _server = server;
        _server.PayloadReceived += Server_PayloadReceived;
        _server.ClientListFull += StartTheRound;

        _engine = new TicTacToeGameEngine();
    }
```

```
private void StartTheRound(object sender, EventArgs e)
{
    _engine.Reset();
    _server.StartGame();
}

private void MakeMove(int[] boardState)
{
    var cellIndex = boardState[0];
    var state = _engine.MakeMove(cellIndex);
    if (state == TicTacToeGameState.Podium)
    {
        _server.ShowPodium(_engine.Winner, _engine.Cells);
    }
    else
    {
        _server.SetCurrentPlayer(_engine.CurrentPlayer,
        _engine.Cells);
    }
}

private void Server_PayloadReceived(object sender,
PayloadEventArgs<GameMessage> e)
{
    var client = (NetworkClient)sender;

    switch (_engine.State)
    {
        case TicTacToeGameState.Playing:
            if (_server.IsCurrentPlayer(client, _engine.
            CurrentPlayer))
```

```
        {
            if (e.Payload.messageType == MessageType.
            ClientMakeMove)
            {
                MakeMove(e.Payload.boardState);
            }
        }
        break;
    case TicTacToeGameState.Podium:
        if (e.Payload.messageType == MessageType.
        ClientPlayAgain)
        {
            StartTheRound(this, EventArgs.Empty);
        }
        else if (e.Payload.messageType == MessageType.
        ClientQuit)
        {
            _server.QuitToTitle();
        }
        break;
    }
  }
}
```

AppController

The last class is the AppController class. The class provides a link between the UI panels used to create the game's visuals as well as instantiation of the server and client. Its main function is to wait for the player to click the Start Server or Join buttons. This action will set off a series of events that will start the server and connect a client, or, in the case of Join, will attempt to join a server.

Open the AppController script file and replace the contents with
Listing 4-48. Save the file.

Listing 4-48. AppController Class

```
using System;
using System.Collections;
using System.Collections.Generic;
using System.Net;
using System.Net.Sockets;
using UnityEngine;

public class AppController : MonoBehaviour
{
    public PanelController _panels;

    private TicTacToeGameServer _gameController;
    private TicTacToeServer _server;

    private List<TicTacToeClientBehaviour> _clients;

    [Tooltip("The port number the Tic Tac Toe server is
    running")]
    public int _port = 9021;

    void Start()
    {
        _clients = new List<TicTacToeClientBehaviour>();

        _panels.GetPanel<MainTitlePanel>().StartServerClicked +=
        StartServer;
        _panels.GetPanel<MainTitlePanel>().JoinServerClicked +=
        JoinServer;
        _panels.GetPanel<StartServerPanel>().CancelClicked +=
        CancelServer;
    }
```

```csharp
private void OnDestroy()
{
    _panels.GetPanel<MainTitlePanel>().StartServerClicked -=
    StartServer;
    _panels.GetPanel<MainTitlePanel>().JoinServerClicked -=
    JoinServer;
}

private void ShowError(string error)
{
    _panels.GetPanel<ErrorPanel>()._text.text = error;
    StartCoroutine(ShowErrorPanel());
}

private void JoinServer(object sender, EventArgs e)
{
    CreateClient();
}

private void CancelServer(object sender, EventArgs e)
{
    StopServer();
}

private void StartServer(object sender, EventArgs e)
{
    if (_server == null)
    {
        _server = new TicTacToeServer(_port);
        _gameController = new TicTacToeGameServer(_server);
        _server.Start();
    }
```

```
    CreateClient(true);
    _panels.ShowPanel(PanelType.StartServer);
}

public void StopServer()
{
    _server?.Stop();
    _gameController = null;
    _server = null;

    _panels.ShowPanel(PanelType.Title);
    ClearClients();
}

private void ClearClients()
{
    foreach (var c in _clients)
    {
        Destroy(c.gameObject);
    }
    _clients.Clear();
}

private void CreateClient(bool local = false)
{
    var go = new GameObject("Client");
    var client = go.AddComponent<TicTacToeClientBehaviour>();
    client._app = this;
    client._board = FindObjectOfType<BoardController>();

    var address = IPAddress.Parse("127.0.0.1");
```

```
    if (!local)
    {
        var userEnteredAddress = _panels.
        GetPanel<MainTitlePanel>().ServerAddress;
        address = GetAddress(userEnteredAddress);
    }

    if (address == IPAddress.None)
    {
        ShowError("Invalid IP Address!");
    }
    else
    {
        var tcpClient = new TcpClient();
        tcpClient.Connect(address, _port);
        client.Connect(tcpClient);
    }

    _clients.Add(client);
}

public IPAddress GetAddress(string ipAddress)
{
    try
    {
        var address = IPAddress.Parse(ipAddress);
        return address;
    }
    catch (FormatException)
    {
        return IPAddress.None;
    }
}
```

```
private IEnumerator ShowErrorPanel(float duration = 3)
{
    _panels.ShowPanel(PanelType.Error);
    yield return new WaitForSeconds(duration);
    _panels.ShowPanel(PanelType.Title);
}
}
```

The CreateClient() method is called if the player is running the server locally or if they are connecting remotely. You need to know the IP address of the server. If you are running the server locally, the default callback of 127.0.0.1 is used.

Now that you have the code for this class, it should be added to the scene. Follow these instructions to add AppController to the scene:

1. In the scene hierarchy, create a new GameObject called AppController.

2. Drag and drop the AppController script file to the AppController game object.

3. With the AppController object selected, drag and drop the TicTacToeUI game object into the AppController's Panels field in the Inspector.

You should now have the object hierarchy shown in Figure 4-16.

Figure 4-16. *The scene hierarchy after creating the AppController object*

When selected, the Inspector should look like Figure 4-17 for the AppController object. Your positional data may be different, but you should have an AppController script attached to it.

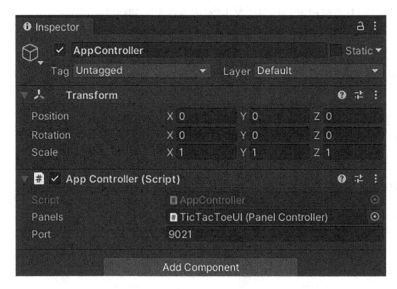

Figure 4-17. *The Inspector showing the components attached to the AppController GameObject*

Now that everything has been written, it's time to play a game of tic-tac-toe!

Running the Game

In order to debug the game, you will need to have two versions running. To do this, you will have to build a version of the game and use that to connect to the one running under the editor.

The first step is to choose the platform to build on. Choose File ➤ Build Settings to access the Build Settings window shown in Figure 4-18. If the current scene isn't in the list, click the Add Open Scenes button.

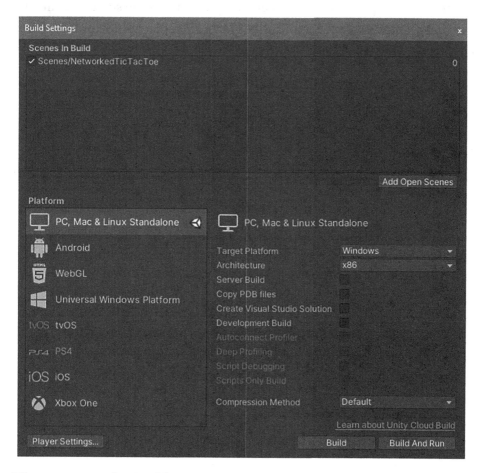

Figure 4-18. *The Build Settings window*

Select the PC, Mac, and Linux Standalone platform and click the Build button. You will be prompted to specify a location. The build will then start.

Run the editor first. This will act as the server for the game. The application you just built will act as the client. Run the client. You may have to use Alt+Tab (also known as Cool Switch) to shift focus between the running game and the Unity Editor.

Figure 4-19 shows the layout of the game being played on a dual monitor. The left side is the client and the right side is the server running in the Unity Editor. Once the applications have been placed side by side, it is easy to see what is happening and play the game.

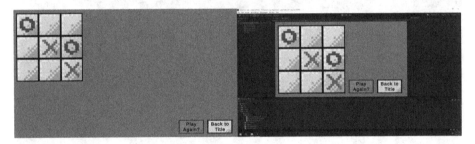

Figure 4-19. *The client and server running on the same machine in side-by-side windows. The client on the left is a standalone executable and the right shows the server running inside the Unity Editor*

Notice that it doesn't take long for the screens to update on a grid click, even though the updates are happening over a network connection. This is because the client and the server are both running on the same machine using the loopback 127.0.0.1 address. Even when playing across the local area network, you shouldn't see much if any delay.

If you run into any problems, there are a couple of troubleshooting points you can try:

- Change the port number of the server. This can be done by changing the port number field on the `AppController GameObject`. The default is 9021.

- Ensure that your firewall is not blocking the port you selected.

- Check the classes and ensure that everything is typed correctly.

There isn't a quick way to change the port number on the client, but I leave that as an exercise for you, dear reader! In the program given, you would need to change the port number and recompile.

Summary

The .Net framework provides a low-level socket connection class in the form of `Socket`. It can be used to establish a connection using a variety of socket types (datagram and stream, for example) and protocols, including TCP. It is easier, however, when using TCP, to use the higher-level classes `TcpClient` and `TcpListener`.

Both synchronous (blocking) and asynchronous (non-blocking) methods are provided to read, write, and wait for connections. It is always better to use the non-blocking methods. This does mean that, in order to complete the operation, you must also code a callback. This is a small price to pay to avoid your game from stuttering or freezing all together.

The `TcpClient` uses a `NetworkStream` to read and write data. It is possible to use a `BinaryWriter`, for example, to write data and a `BinaryReader` to read data from this stream. It is often easier using the `BeginWrite()` and `BeginRead()` methods. These methods allow a state object to be passed to allow context to be established in the callback.

For example, when ending a `write` the state object would be the client performing the `write` operation.

Reading or writing large amounts of data might require multiple operations. This can be done by having a smaller reception buffer and filling a larger buffer. You will need to include some way in your protocol to inform the receiver what size of payload you intend to send.

At the end of this chapter, you built on your knowledge to create a TCP version of Tic-Tac-Toe for two players, utilizing the `TcpClient` and `TcpListener` classes. You used wrappers to abstract the client connections and the server to make it easier for the game code to interact with the underlying networking code.

CHAPTER 5

Networking Issues

The previous chapters covered multiple concepts related to network fundamentals. Those fundamentals work great and provide a great deal of support when working with any network architecture.

Since games are similar to software to a certain extent, those concepts should work fine with games as well. But things start getting completed when you consider a zero lag system and authority issues in case of discrepancies. This chapter covers these networking caveats and their workarounds.

Authoritative Servers

To understand the concept of authoritative servers, let's look at the traditional communication method of a chat system. Chat apps usually display messages in order of time stamps. If two people send a message at the same time, the app takes the message that reached the server first, making it more like a race condition. This method is good but not scalable. If the number of messages grows, the app will not be able to sort the messages, as it might not have enough time differences.

That is the case with most games since they usually work with UDP data packets and need to be in sync with other players. Whose copy of the data is valid? This issue becomes even more complicated when it's a P2P network.

The original version of this chapter was revised. A correction to this chapter is available at https://doi.org/10.1007/978-1-4842-7358-6_9

© Sloan Kelly and Khagendra Kumar 2022, corrected publication 2022
S. Kelly and K. Kumar, *Unity Networking Fundamentals*,
https://doi.org/10.1007/978-1-4842-7358-6_5

In turn-based games, it is usually much easier to give the server the final authority. With real-time games, that design is usually a good place to start, but once you add latency, the movement/actions of the gamers will feel unresponsive. You can add some sort of "hide delay," which allows customers to touch their character or units quickly to solve that problem, but then you have to deal with reconciliation issues when the client and game state servers start to differ. Most of the time, that it is okay, because you can pop or lerp the things the client touched instead of authorization. But when there is an avatar player, for example, that solution is not acceptable. You have to start to empower the client in some of the actions. Now you have to reconcile more games on the server, and then give yourself the opportunity to "cheat" with a bad client. If you care more about these reconciliation issues and try to fix them, you'll usually have to apply predictive logic to compensate for the issues. This where all the teleport/dupe/any bug/cheat efforts come from.

You can simply start with a model where all the clients have control over their own stuff and ignore the cheating problem (which works in a few cases). But now you are at risk of having a major impact on the game's performance if that client goes out, or "falls backwards to match the simulation." Effectively, all player games will end up paying the consequences for the client who is lagging behind or doing poorly, by waiting for the backlog to catch, or have the game state they control without syncing.

Synchronous or Asynchronous

Multiplayer games rely on players interacting with each other, which generates a lot of data about every player. That data needs to be shared, depending on the type of game the player is playing.

The game developer must decide how the data will be shared with other players—whether it will be shared synchronously or asynchronously.

Synchronous games are the type of games in which players all play at the same time. To guarantee a good game-playing experience, you must ensure that all the players' data is shared in real-time with all the other players.

A common strategy is to ensure that all players work in the same game state and agree on the player's input list (one of the types described previously). The game simulation game is then played harmoniously on all machines. This means that the simulation must be precisely aligned or the games will be out of sync. This is both easier and harder than it might seem. It's easy because the game is just code, and code works very well when it has the same input (even generators with random numbers). It is difficult in two cases:

- When you accidentally use random play without imitating your game

- When you are using a float

The first one is fixed by having strict rules/guarantees about which RNG (Random Number Generator) game systems are used. The latter is solved by not using a float. (Floats actually have two problems—they work very differently based on the planned performance of your project and they work inconsistently with other different processors.) StarCraft/World of Warcraft and any game that offers "replay" may use this model. In fact, having a replay system is a great way to check that your RNGs are synced. Roleplay games are very good examples of these kinds of games.

Asynchronous games doesn't require that all the game state data be shared with every player. One example are turn-based games such as online pool, online Ludo, or online Carrom. The players don't play the game at the same time. More than one player plays the game and the data of each player is shared with the other players.

In an asynchronous solution, game management is simply spread to the other clients over and over again. Clients take that data and add it to their game state (and normally do some simple tricks until they get the next update). This is where UDP becomes a viable option, because it infects the entire game state very quickly. However, discarding a portion of those updates is not necessary. For games that have a small game empire (such as Earthquake and World of Warcraft), this is usually a simple solution.

Planning Multiplayer Games

Games are complex pieces of software and there are a lot of places where they can go wrong. When you start developing your game, you will usually follow some software development principles to ensure that the game works properly. There is usually a design stage whereby you design the system architecture and services architecture to optimize the development and performance of the game.

From a software engineering point of view, a multiplayer game needs to share each and every movement of one player with all the other players in real-time. This can be a very complicated process. Luckily, you can focus on a few game-specific parameters while designing a system for your multiplayer game, such as the following:

- **Loading data**: Every computer will have the same models and graphics, and just the names and locations will be transmitted over the Internet. If every player can customize their own character, you have to move this data around.

- **Cheating**: Should you worry about this? Can you trust what each customer says? Otherwise, the server-side line will look different than your customer's perspective. Consider this simple case whereby each of your 10 players has a different movement speed due to the force of the electric current. To reduce cheating, you have to calculate how far each player can go between connection updates from the server. Otherwise, players can hack when they are fast and nothing can stop them. If a player consistently slows down faster than expected or jumps once, the server will reset to the closest possible location, as it could be a clock issue or a one-time communication interruption. However, if a player stays as fast as possible, it would be wise to take them out of the game. The more numbers, the more parts of the game mode you can double-check on the server. The game will be more consistent and cheating will be more difficult.

- **Local server**: No matter what the game looks like you will want one player to start the game and use it as a server. This is a lot easier than trying to manage other clouds. In the absence of a server, you need to use the protocol for resolving disputes between two machines with incompatible gaming consoles.

Once you have planned and thought through your pipeline and the techniques that you will be using in your multiplier game, you need to look deeper into the technology and technicalities.

Game Lag

Anyone developing an application that uses the Internet or that has networking capabilities must consider two key things that can affect the performance of the application. If the application relies completely on the Internet, it might become unusable because of these two issues:

- Bandwidth
- Latency

Bandwidth

Bandwidth is the maximum amount of data that can pass through the network at a given time. Consider it like lanes on the highway, whereby only a certain number of vehicles can drive on them at one time.

Bandwidth should not be confused with the speed of the Internet, although it does affect the speed indirectly. The more available bandwidth there is, the more data can be downloaded synchronously.

In other words, bandwidth is the volume of data moving at any instant in time.

Even though bandwidth measures data volume over a network, it does not speculate about how data is moving from one node of the network to another. As data travels through the network (via Ethernet, coax, fiber, or any other connection media), bandwidth turns a blind eye toward the network speed.

For bandwidth, it can be helpful to imagine a hose connected via a pipe or a tube to a water tank. This water tank can upload data at an infinite speed and has an unlimited bandwidth (which is realistically not possible). Speed at which the water is flowing is the Internet speed and the volume of water that is coming out of the hose at any given instance is the bandwidth. If you increase the diameter of hose, the volume of water coming out will increase, but the speed of water might not be affected.

Data often moves through multiple networks or computers, and the terminating points of these are usually the personal devices, such as computer, phone, or laptop. If we backtrack the connections, we will find that bandwidth is very high for backbone systems of the Internet. For example, bandwidth available via India's TIER-I provider is more than 20+Tbps. Because of this, you commonly don't get slow data if you have more bandwidth available with your ISP.

How Bandwidth Works

The more bandwidth there is, the more data can be sent and received at once. The wider the hose, the more water can pass through. Likewise, the higher the capacity of the connection or pipeline, the more data can pass through in a second.

Most of these expenses are paid by the end consumers. The higher the bandwidth you want for your connection, the higher the charges for that connection.

Bandwidth vs. Speed

Many people confuse bandwidth and speed. The main part of the confusion is due to the way they are portrayed in advertisements for high speed, when they actually mean high bandwidth. In fact, speed means how fast data can be sent and received and bandwidth means how much data can be sent and received. Fiber-optic based connections are close to the speed of light, so the bandwidth will define how your experience is.

Why Bandwidth Is Important

For connectivity in homes and offices, bandwidth requirements vary based on use. Most homes need less bandwidth compared to businesses, because the latter may have hundreds of computers connected to the Internet, all with time-critical information to be carried back and forth. Low bandwidth in this case would choke the Internet. In conclusion, high bandwidth is required when multiple devices are connected to the Internet simultaneously.

How to Measure Bandwidth

Bandwidth is usually measured in bits per second, not in bytes per second, which is why there is a difference of symbols (Mbps and MBPS). Bits are represented with a lowercase b, whereas bytes are represented with an uppercase B. Most modern systems have very high transmission power and can send and receive millions of bits per second:

```
[8 bit = 1 Byte]
```

Bandwidth come in two types:

- *Symmetrical*

    Networks that can upload and download the same amount of data at a time are known as symmetrical connections.

    These types of connections are very common on wired connections such as fiber optic connections.

- *Asymmetrical*

    Networks that are not configured for uploading and downloading the same amount of data at a time are known as asymmetrical connections.

    These connections are very common in wireless connections, such as mobile data and satellite Internet. These types of connections are used in home-based connections, as not a lot of people upload huge amounts of data over the Internet.

Performance Factors

There are a lot of factors that can impact the performance of a network. A lot of them have to do with the activities and the way the network is organized. For example, if the devices are connected to a same access point without proper rules about how the traffic should be handled by the access point or router, there may be packet loss and network congestion, which adversely affect the network's performance.

Demand on Demand

Demand on demand is a marketing term that can be understood by VOD (Video on Demand). As the name suggests, video is available whenever there is a demand for it. It may be via OTT platforms or streaming websites.

Corporate Internet connections are dedicated lines and are sold at fixed prices. In the case of domestic connections, most people are unaware of their bandwidth requirements. How much bandwidth do they need? They often opt for plans according to their budget or based on the sales representative's recommendation. In many situations, they buy more than they need. Even if they need it, they may not be saturating the bandwidth 24*7, allowing the bandwidth to be shared by other people with the same plans.

According to my research, ISPs opt for a 1:50 ratio. This means that for every 1Mbps of bandwidth, they will have 50 people on it, as not all of them will be using it at one instance. Whenever that happens, you get a slow experience.

Latency

What is network latency? Is it important? Why does it differ a lot? Figure 5-1 is a graphical representation of latency.

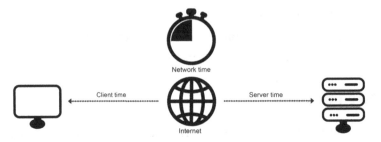

Figure 5-1. *Latency representation*

Latency can simply be considered a delay. Delay and latency are used interchangeably in literature but not in networking terminology. Latency in networking is measured as the roundtrip delay, i.e., the time it takes the data packet to travel from the source to the destination and to come back.

This roundtrip delay is an important measure, as computers use the TCP/IP protocol, whereby the computer sends data to its destination and then waits for its acknowledgement before sending new data. Thus, roundtrip delay can have a significant impact on network performance.

Latency is the time taken by the system/network on the users' action over the network for a resulting response. Network delays refer to the delays directly in the network. I general terms, latency is the time taken by the website or service to respond over the Internet once the user clicks the button and the appropriate result is shown to them.

Although data travels at the speed of light, the distance can still affect the system and cause delays. Latency often comes from the infrastructure required by the Internet itself, which cannot be completely eliminated. However, this infrastructure can be reduced and optimized for better latency.

What Causes Network Latency?

There are many factors that cause delays over networks. One of the main causes is distance, mostly the distance between the client and server. If a website is hosted in the United States and the client is in India, the request has to travel the entire distance and come back.

For data traveling at the speed of light, this doesn't seem very far, but it can result in a few milliseconds of added delay. This affect is compounded, as most websites have at least five network connections for CSS and JavaScript files. There is also the processing time for all those files.

Nowadays, web pages incorporate complex structures and a huge amount of data in terms of graphics and the downloadable content from multiple sources, so web developers include techniques like lazy load to deliver the website faster. But if the web page has many graphical elements, it could still take longer to load.

In addition, the way web pages are designed can also lead to slower performance. Web pages that incorporate large amounts of heavy content or downloadable content from third parties can be slow, because browsers have to download large files to display them. Users close to the datacenter hosting the website they are accessing may be fine, but if the website has many high-definition images (for example), there may still be a delay as the images upload.

All of this can be summarized as follows:

- The connection type and types of hardware can significantly affect network delays.

- The distance between the client and server can affect the delay.

- Infrastructure elements such as router switches and exchange also add delay caused by processing time.

- I/O delay will also add up, as it takes milliseconds to fetch data from storage devices.

Now let's explore some common problems that can add delay from the client and server sides.

Distribution Delay

This is the time required by the data to reach its destination, which is a function of the speed at which the signal is being transmitted and the distance it must travel.

Delivery Delay

The time required for a file/web page to collect the data packet from the transmission. This is dependent on the data packet size and the transmission speed.

Processing Delay

The time taken by the system to process the data packet for errors and integrity, and then to forward that packet to the destination.

Line Delay

The delay caused by being in the queue for processing to happen.

A delay between the client and the server is the total sum of all the calculated delays. Distribution time is defined by the distance and location of the signal. As you will see, the speed of distribution is often within the normal range of the speed of light, whereas the delivery delay is caused by the availability of data at the relay server after processing.

As an example, say that you want to transfer a 10MB file over two destinations: 1 Mbps and 100 Mbps. It will take 10 seconds to put the entire file "on the phone" at the 1 Mbps link and only 0.1 seconds at the 100 Mbps link.

The next step is to check the data packet for its next steps from its information header. First the router will check the data integrity, then it will look for the next step, information from header. Most of these things are done via hardware processing, which is usually slower than the data transmission rate. Therefore, the data packets start queuing up in the incoming buffer. Time spent in that buffer is called a linear delay.

Every data packet will have multiple instances of these types of delays, depending on the distance between the server and the client and the number of routers or hops the data packet takes. The more devices or routers there are, the longer the delay will be and the longer the line delay will be as well.

Speed of Light and Latency

Nothing can travel faster than light and data packets carried through light inside optical fibers are traveling at that same speed. This creates a limitation on the rate that data can be transmitted.

However, light can travel at a speed of 299 million meters/sec or 186K miles/hour. This speed is in a vacuum; light carrying data packets cannot travel at these max speeds. The speed at which data can travel in copper wire is much lower than in optical fiber. Table 5-1 outlines these speeds.

Table 5-1. *Signal Latencies*

Route	Distance	Time (Light in Vacuum)	Time (Light in Fiber)	RTT
New York to San Francisco	4148 KM	14ms	21ms	42ms
New York to London	5585 KM	19ms	28ms	56ms
New York to Sydney	15993 KM	53ms	80ms	160ms
Equatorial circumference	40075 KM	133.7ms	200ms	400ms

The speed of light is fast but it is not instant; it still takes more than 150 milliseconds to travel from New York to Sydney and back. The data in Table 5-1 assumes that packets travel through optical fiber in a large circle between cities, which is rare. In most cases, the route taken by data packets has a very large number of hops in between and can take longer to reach its destination. Each hop will add delay, and the actual roundtrip time will increase significantly. Considering everything, the roundtrip time can be 200-300ms, which is really good.

Humans are not very sensitive to delays in milliseconds; however, research suggests that a delay of 100-200ms can be detected by the human brain. When the 300ms delay mark is crossed, the human brain sees it as lazy. If it reaches 1000ms, (1 second), the human brain will start questing the connection speed, the system response, the connectivity, and so on.

The point of all this information is that you should try to make content available for users as close to them as possible, in order to reduce the delay and latency and keep it under 100ms. To be successful in reducing the latency of the network, you must carefully manage it and provide a clear, less congested path.

Last Mile Latency

You might be astonished to know that most latency is added when the connection is about to reach your home office, not in underground cables or when crossing continents. This is referred to as the *last mile latency*. To connect to your home, your ISP will use wires with the router at its exchange and might add several hops along the line to reduce installation and maintenance costs. Sometime these can add up to hundreds of milliseconds of latency.

According to the FCC, global-based broadband service has three performance ratings:

- 10-20ms is good

- 15-40ms is moderate

- 30-65ms is a DSL connection

This latency of 10-65ms is to the closest server inside the main ISP network, before the data packet is delivered to its final destination. The FCC report mainly focuses on United States broadband. However, the last mile connectivity is a challenge for all Internet service providers in all geographic locations. Ironically, this the area where most Internet bandwidth is affected as well.

If you want to know about latency in your network, you can run a simple `traceroute` command in a shell. It will tell you how many hops there are before reaching the destination. See Figure 5-2.

```
C:\>tracert google.com

Tracing route to google.com [2404:6800:4009:801::200e]
over a maximum of 30 hops:

  1     2 ms     1 ms     1 ms  2402:3a80:46a:935d::bb
  2    69 ms    31 ms    32 ms  2402:3a80:46a:935d:0:6e:9f25:ac40
  3     *        *        *     Request timed out.
  4    71 ms    29 ms    27 ms  fd00:0:2:2::4
  5    70 ms    34 ms    29 ms  fd00:abcd:abcd:232::2
  6    44 ms    29 ms    36 ms  2400:5200:1800:11::2
  7    73 ms    38 ms    39 ms  2001:4860:1:1::6eb
  8    41 ms    41 ms    39 ms  2001:4860:1:1::150e
  9    66 ms    38 ms    33 ms  2404:6800:8075::1
 10   138 ms    44 ms    32 ms  2001:4860:0:e00::1
 11   136 ms    34 ms    40 ms  2001:4860:0:e00::2
 12   102 ms    59 ms    59 ms  2001:4860::9:4001:7733
 13    61 ms    60 ms    53 ms  2001:4860:0:115b::1
 14    99 ms    83 ms    66 ms  2001:4860:0:1::11c1
 15   101 ms    49 ms    50 ms  bom07s10-in-x0e.1e100.net [2404:6800:4009:801::200e]
```

Figure 5-2. *Traceroute maps for connecting servers*

As the last mile doesn't have a distance-based limitation, it usually varies with the ISP. Some ISPs have a small service area, whereas other giants have a very huge service area. Depending on the technology and topology used by your ISP, the quality of your connection will be different. To get better service and speed, always research the ISPs in your area.

Client-Side Prediction and Server Reconciliation

A basic implementation of user action prediction and server reconciliation leads to a delay between the commands given by the user in the game and the changes reflected onscreen, as well as the changes propagated to other players. For example, consider a player pressing arrow keys to move their character, but it takes 500 milliseconds for the character to start moving. This happens because the command/button press information takes time to reach the server. The server must process the input and calculate the new vector position of the player. Once that is done, the update will be sent to the player. See Figure 5-3.

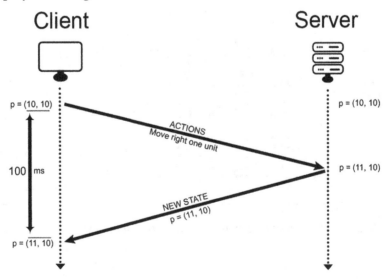

Figure 5-3. *Representation of network delay*

In an online gaming environment where delays matter a lot, a delay of even a few seconds may make the game feel unresponsive. In a worse-case scenario, players might leave the game. We must find ways to reduce or even eliminate this problem.

Client-Side Predictions

Almost all online games will have some cheaters playing the game and most gaming servers are configured in a way to process valid requests. (Assuming cheaters camouflage their requests as legit requests.) This means that the input received by the server will be processed and the game will be updated as expected. If a player was at (10,10), for example, and the right arrow key is pressed, the player's new position after a server update will be (11,10). Since these behaviors are predictable, you can use this to your advantage. Assume, for example, that you are playing a game and the character animation plays for 100ms. You have a latency of 100ms, so you have total latency of 200ms. See Figure 5-4.

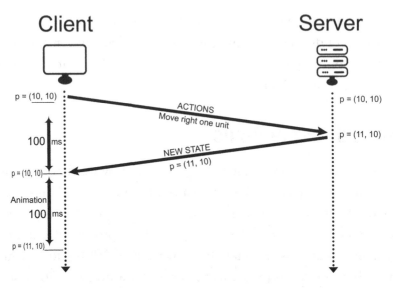

Figure 5-4. *Network delay plus animation delay*

Let's assume that whatever input is sent to the server is executed successfully. In that case, the client can predict the game state according to the game environment, after the input has been processed by the server. This way, the prediction made by client will be correct most of the time.

So rather than sending the input to the server and waiting for the result, you can send the input directly to the game and get the input, assuming that the server sent the report using a prediction method and you can wait for the server to respond accordingly. See Figure 5-5.

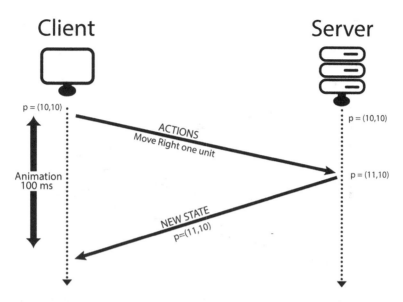

Figure 5-5. *Playing animation during network delay*

This way, you don't have a delay between the player's actions onscreen while the server is still in control (if there is a discrepancy in the data, the server data will be considered valid).

Synchronization Issues

In the previous example, we carefully chose a number that reduced the mathematical complexities. However, it is far from an ideal case. So now let's say that the delay between the server and the user is 250ms and the animation plays for 100ms. If the player makes a move two times by pressing the appropriate button, Figure 5-6 shows how this process might proceed.

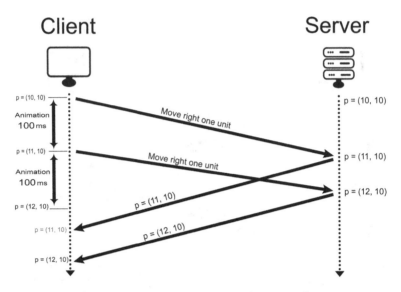

Figure 5-6. *Predictive state mismatch with an authoritative server*

The delay is 250ms, so we can consider t = 250ms. Whenever there is movement in the game, a new game state will be there. Now let's say the player status after the move is (12,10) on the player's computer. The server will assume that the player is at (11,10), as the player made two movements and the server needs to compute for two movements. After completing the first calculation, the player will go back to (11,10) at 350ms, but after processing the second command, the server will bring the player back to (12,10).

From the player's perspective, they made a move in the game and then started waiting for something. But in the meantime, the character was skipping left and right because of the server calculation, which is unacceptable.

Server Reconciliation

There are ways to fix this problem. One of the key approaches is to have a priority update. This means that if the player is playing the game, the server will send the updates to the game. That way, if the server has not finished processing all the commands from the player, it will not update that player. It should update the player after completing the commands.

This is not very difficult to implement. First, the client uses a sequence number found in the header information of each request sent to it. When the server needs to respond, it keeps the sequence data inside the header. See Figure 5-7.

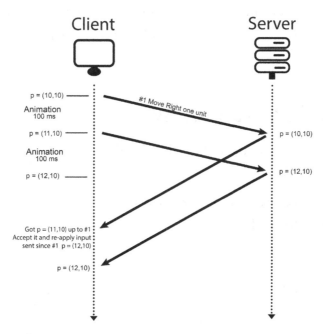

Figure 5-7. *Client prediction and server reconciliation*

Once this method is implemented, the server will respond differently. When t =250ms, the server might respond. For your first request, for example, the player should be at (11,10) and then for your second request, the player should be at (12,10), which is correct.

215

Further Steps

All these examples are from player movement and these same principles can be applied to any other logic as well.

Games are very complex pieces of software and are very difficult to develop. along When players get excited during the game, their movements can affect other players, such as scoring or dying in the game. It's best to let the server verify whether the player is dead or not to avoid conflicts.

It doesn't matter which kind of player is in the games player base, whether there are bots or hackers playing the game. The server data might not match the client game. This might not be a great concern in a single-player player game, but can be of concern when a lot of players are playing the game.

Getting Ping from Unity

The following code snippet returns the ping time taken by the application to complete an RTT:

```
Ping ping = new Ping("<<Server IP>>);
While(!ping.isDone){
    Yield;
    }
return ping.time;
```

Summary

This chapter started by covering problems with conventional networking that you have to handle before you can focus on multiplayer game development. The chapter then discussed synchronous and asynchronous games, which are types of multiplayer games that buffer a lot when implementing the system.

Lastly, the chapter covered bandwidth, latency, and ping and how to handle these shortcomings with server reconciliation and client prediction.

CHAPTER 6

Develop a Maze Shooter

In this chapter, you will learn how to create a multiplayer game. The chapter goes through the key steps required to create a multiplayer game. The process is divided into multiple steps.

Before we jump right into multiplayer games, let's look at some keywords used frequently in multiplayer games.

Lobby

A lobby is a waiting area in any building. Similar to that concept, a *lobby* is the matchmaking area of a multiplayer game.

Matchmaking

The room allocation or *matchmaking* process can be handled by allocating players to different rooms using matchmaking algorithms.

One of the simplest ways is to allocate on a first-come/first-serve basis, but there are many more sophisticated algorithms to ensure a better match. These algorithms are similar to matchmaking algorithms , or algorithms used by dating websites. The key concept is to match a player with another player of a similar level so that the match is fair. Most online

S. Kelly and K. Kumar, *Unity Networking Fundamentals*,
https://doi.org/10.1007/978-1-4842-7358-6_6

multiplayer service providers use multiple KPIs to match players, such as network speed, past scores, game winning history, and so on. Combining these and more details helps create a rank and using this rank, algorithms create a group of players who are suited to play together.

Spawn/Respawn

The process of appearing or reappearing in the game, either at the beginning of the game or after dying in the game.

Spawn Point

The room or the area of a game where players respawn after death.

Introducing the RPG Game

This section is a hands-on, step-by-step tutorial for creating a simple multiplayer game.

This game is a primitive representation of RPG shooting game that happens inside a Maze environment. It's created this way for the sake of simplicity and understanding and can be extended to a complete multiplayer game.

The Game's Story

The game starts with a maze and the player in a certain start position. Enemies are placed inside the maze as well. The goal of the player is to reach the end of the maze and collect the treasure to finish the game.

Game Prerequisites

To create this game, you must have:

- A basic understanding of Unity and game development in Unity.

- A basic understanding of object-oriented programming using C#.

- An understanding of the material covered in Chapters 1-5.

- Downloaded the Unity Hub and at least one Unity Editor (preferably 2020.3 or higher).

- Git Bash installed in your system, as it is utilized in the Unity multiplayer setup.

This tutorial project uses a mid-level networking library provided by Unity. Unity provides this mid-level networking library with most of the methods and communications system already programmed. As you learned in the previous chapters, creating a socket connect is a complicated process.

Creating an entire system for a multiplayer game can be very tedious.

High-level multiplayer libraries can come in handy because they include code for multiple subsystems such as:

- Network management

- Network behavior

- Message handling

- High-purpose deserialization of data

- Object management

- Game state synchronization

- Server class, client class, connection class, and so on

Section 1: Creating the Project and Setting Up Unity

To create a Unity project, you need to open the Unity Hub. This section assumes that you have Unity Hub and Unity Editor installed.

Open Unity Hub and create a new project. Select 3D as the template and then create a 3D project, as shown in Figure 6-1.

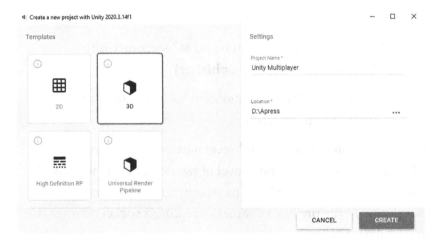

Figure 6-1. *Create a 3D project*

After creating the project, create a plane by choosing Game Object ➤ 3D ➤ Plane. You will then get the screen shown in Figure 6-2.

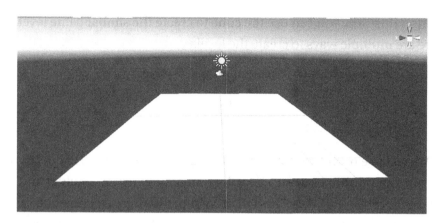

Figure 6-2. *Create a plane*

Now create a simple maze level using the simple cube primitives. For this reference, apply the maze design texture on the Plane gameObject using a material. After you do this, you'll get the view shown in Figure 6-3.

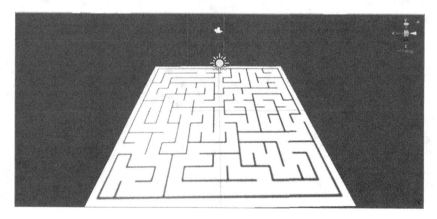

Figure 6-3. *Maze texture*

After this step, you can use the cube to create the similar game level. There are multiple ways to create the level:

- Use a digital content creation (DCC) tool

- Use pro-builder inside Unity

- Use primitives

We will use primitives to create the level in this example. (For details on using pro-builder, refer to the Unity documentation for Pro-Builder and for DCC tools, refer to the Asset Import section of the Unity Documentation.)

To create a cube, choose Game Object ➤ 3D ➤ Cube and then use the Move [icon] and Scale [icon] tools to place the object properly.

After creating the cube, you can remove the texture of maze from the plane and add a grass texture; see Figure 6-4.

Figure 6-4. *The maze with a grass texture*

Section 2: Downloading and Installing MLAPI

To install MLAPI, you need Git Bash installed on your computer. If it's not installed, be sure to install it. It requires you to restart your PC. After that, you can continue from this same position.

To install the MLAPI package, you need to use Package Manager. Choose Window ➤ Package Manager to access it. From this Package Manager, click the + button and select Add Package from Git URL. Then enter `https://github.com/Unity-Technologies/com.unity.multiplayer.mlapi.git?path=/com.unity.multiplayer.mlapi#release/0.1.0` as the Git URL in the provided field. Then click Add. After successful installation, the Package Manager will appear as shown in Figure 6-5.

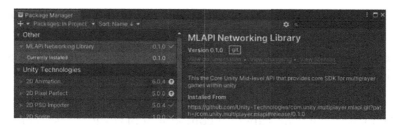

Figure 6-5. *The Package Manager*

Section 3: Programming with MLAPI

During this step, you need to add your player to the game. Since you are creating a multiplayer game, you also need to finalize a few things in this game. You need to make a few decisions and lay down some ground rules before you move any further.

Game decisions:

- The game will have an authoritative server which will control everything.

- The first player to start the game will host the game on a local network. Others will join as clients.

Section 3.1 Adding a Network Manager

To begin development of this multiplayer game, you need to create a Network Manager which will be responsible for creating/spawning the players. You will create an empty game object. You can name this object anything, but for simplicity, let's call it the Network Manager.

Now select the Network Manager and go to the Inspector tab to add some components that will allow this Network Manager to act like a real Network Manager. Add the Network Manager available in the MLAPI group; to do this go to the Inspector window and choose Add Component ➤ MLAPI ➤ Network Manager.

After this step, you need to configure network transport. From this Inspector panel, you will find Select Transport option in which you need to select a transport layer. Select UNet Transport. After selecting UNet Transport, it will add another component of UNet Transport to the Network Manager game object. The UNet Transport object should not be deleted and it should look Figure 6-6.

Figure 6-6. *The UNet Transport object*

After you complete all the steps properly, the Inspector window of the Network Manager should look like Figure 6-7.

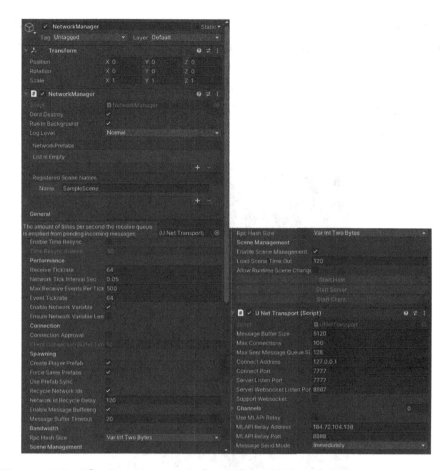

Figure 6-7. *The Inspector window of the Network Manager*

Section 3.2

Once the Network Manager is ready, you can create your player using any prefab. Let's use a capsule as a player. To create a capsule, choose Game Object 3D ➤ Capsule.

Once the player is ready, you need to add some MLAPI components so that it can be utilized properly. To do that, you will again add a network object component to this game object. To add the component, select the player game object from the Inspector window and choose Add Component ➤ MLAPI ➤ Network Object. After this, your Inspector window should look like Figure 6-8.

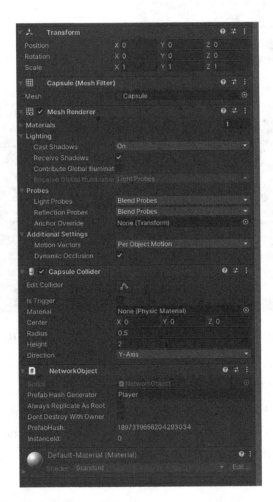

Figure 6-8. *The Inspector window*

Player Movement

In order to add movement to your characters, you create a first-person controller for the player. Since it's an authoritative server, the player's movement should be authorized by the server. This movement should be part of the networking library.

To make the movement part of the network, the player prefab should have another component called networkTransform.

Choose Add Component ➤ MLAPI ➤ Network Transform.

It should be noted that the player prefab will have two MLAPI components—NetworkObject and NetworkTransform—and an FPS controller for the player controls. After all these components, the Inspector panel should look Figure 6-9.

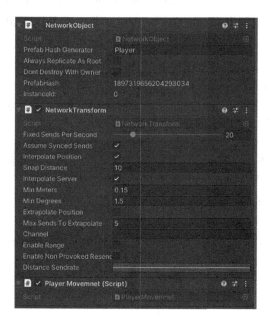

Figure 6-9. *The updated Inspector panel*

Now you need to configure the Network Manager, as it will be responsible for creating a player once the game starts. The server will not be able to control things that are not created by the Network Manager.

For this, you must save the player as a prefab first; drag the player from the Hierarchy to the Project window to create a prefab. After creating the prefab, you can safely delete the player from the hierarchy.

Section 3.3

To make the Game Manager work for this game, you need the UI to start the game. You can create simple buttons called Host and Client using Unity Canvas.

To create a canvas, choose gameObject ➤ UI ➤ Canvas. To add buttons and text input options, first select the Canvas and then choose Game Object ➤ UI ➤ Button. The button will then be created as a child component of the Canvas. Inside this button, you will have a text component. You can change the name of the button by selecting the text component from the hierarchy. In the Inspector window, change the Button Text to **HOST,** which will start the server (see Figure 6-10).

Figure 6-10. *Changing the button text*

Similarly, you can create a Join button which will be used by clients to join the server; see Figure 6-11.

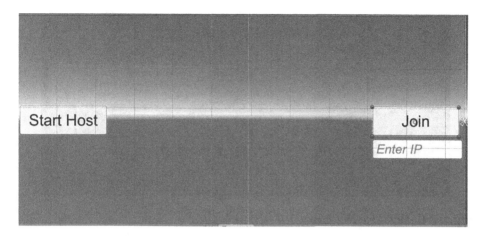

Figure 6-11. *Create a Join button*

To manage the UI and the connections, you can create an empty game object and call it connectionManager. In this connection manager, add a new component script to add functionality to this UI. Create a script by choosing Add Component ➤ New Script ➤ ConnectionManager.

Section 3.4

To open the connectionManager script, double-click it. It should open by default in the code editor. If not, you can configure the text editor by choosing Edit ➤ Preferences ➤ External Tools and finding External Script Editor. Select your favorite tool from the dropdown or browse the Launcher Location. See Figure 6-12.

231

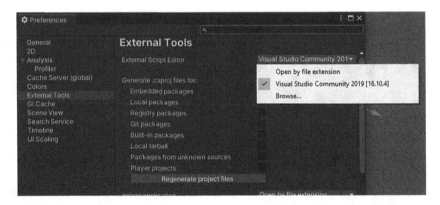

Figure 6-12. *Use the External Script Editor*

After opening the script in the text editor, the first thing you have to do is import the MLAPI Library in the code. You will write this using MLAPI at the start of the file.

```
using MLAPI;
```

To connect and control the UI panel's visibility, create a `public` variable of `GameObject` type and name it `ConnectionPanelUI`; see Figure 6-13.

```
public class ConnectionManager : MonoBehaviour
{
    public GameObject ConnectionPanelUI;
```

Figure 6-13. *Create the ConnectionPanelUI variable*

Now go back to the Unity Editor and add the Canvas to this public field. You do this by dragging the Canvas `GameObject` to this field. Or you can click the circle-looking symbol at the corner of the field and select Canvas from that dropdown. See Figure 6-14.

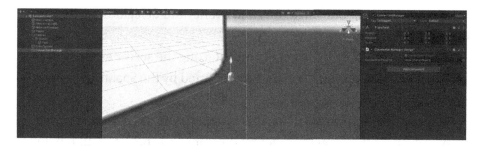

Figure 6-14. *Add the Canvas to the public field*

After that, you can control the canvas with the ConenctionPanelUI variable. To create a button functionality for the Host button, create a public StartHost function as follows.

```
public void StartHost()
    {
        ConnectionPanelUI.gameObject.SetActive(false);
        NetworkManager.Singleton.ConnectionApprovalCallback +=
        ApprovalCheck;
        NetworkManager.Singleton.StartHost(SpawnCharacter(),
        Quaternion.identity);
    }
```

This code creates a function named StartHost which runs whenever the user clicks the Host button on the screen. When the user clicks the Host button, it will hide the canvas, for which we are using setActive(false).

NetworkManager is a singleton class that's available inside the MLAPI library. We are using that instance of that class to pass the parameters to start the hosting server. In this case, it takes the spawnCharacter function and its position.

ApprovalCheck determines if the networking setup is correct in the UNet Transport settings. It also determines if the clients can join the game or not.

233

To learn more about singletons and events and delegates, read more about C# references.

This code is hiding the UI panel and starting the server as the host; it's also spawning the player at the position defined by the SpawnCharacter() function.

To provide the approval using this function, you must set up the password. To do that, you must define the approval check function being called via the delegate event.

This uses a hardcoded password for simplicity of code. With this change, the code for the host will change, as the host must have an authentication system to authenticate a new player.

Once the StartHost button is clicked, its requesting connection approval calls back to check and authenticate the password.

```
private void ApprovalCheck(byte[] connectionData, ulong
ClientID, NetworkManager.ConnectionApprovedDelegate callback)
    {
        bool approve = System.Text.Encoding.ASCII.
        GetString(connectionData) == "Password1234";
        callback(true, null, approve, SpawnCharacter(),
        Quaternion.identity);
    }
```

Joining the Game

To join any online game, you must know the IP address of the server so that the game can connect and share its data. For this, you must enter the IP address when you want to join the server.

By default, the localhost IP is 127.0.0.1 so you can keep this IP hardcoded in your game. Since this is a networking game, one server can host multiple games. The game server will have some type of authentication system to allow and block players.

After receiving the callback, the host will start the game. It's time for the client to connect to the player. You pass the IP address from the UI of the game as a dynamic string value to the code by using InputOnValueChangeEvent().

To join the game, the host and client must know the IP. You pass the IP address to the UNetTransport layer of MLAPI, which is the low-level networking library for Unity. To do this, you will again set a reference to NetworkManager and its UNetTransport component.

```
transport = NetworkManager.Singleton.
GetComponent<UNetTransport>();
```

Once you get the reference to UNetTransport, you can set the IP for the client connection.

```
public void Join()
    {
        transport = NetworkManager.Singleton.
        GetComponent<UNetTransport>();
        transport.ConnectAddress = ipAddress;
        ConnectionPanelUI.gameObject.SetActive(false);
        NetworkManager.Singleton.NetworkConfig.ConnectionData =
        System.Text.Encoding.ASCII.GetBytes("Password1234");
        NetworkManager.Singleton.StartClient();
    }
```

This code implements the Network Manager as a singleton pattern named singleton. This is defined along with MonoBehaviour. This same singleton contains information about the host, server, and client.

You will call these methods in the onGUI() method of Unity to render it in runtime.

MLAPI Event Messaging

To understand MLAPI event messaging, this section uses a shooting mechanism example. For this to happen, you must write object-pooling code for a bullet.

Using Remote Procedural Calls (RPCs)

Remote procedural calls are utilized by network communication interfaces to share information from the client to the server and vice versa.

Especially with an authoritative server configuration, nothing moves without the server's consent and most of the commands given by the player need to be executed by the server. In these cases, the commands' communication can be established by RPC. For example, if a player has to shoot, the player will initialize a [ServerRPC] so that the server can shoot on behalf of the player. Similarly, the server will send the data back and the gameObject can receive that data using [ClientRPC] params.

For more params like this in MLAPI, see the "Event Messaging" reference in the documentation.

Working with Bullets in Multiplayer Games

In a normal game, once a bullet is shot, the player or the Game Manager takes control of the bullet and decides the next step. This works fine in single player games, as everything is local. But this is not the case with multiplayer games. Bullets cannot be managed by the Game Manager because all the players have a Game Manager that's managing all local changes. Since the server is the highest authority and it's managing all the players, control of the bullet should go to the server.

But that's also not possible because the server will have to do a lot of computation and it may not be able to manage the game properly.

One of the most common approaches is to share bullet details to all clients. Then the client can compute for itself and the server can just monitor it.

```
public GameObject gunbullet;
    public Transform gun;
    // Update is called once per frame
    void Update()
    {
        if(IsLocalPlayer)
        {
            if(Input.GetMouseButtonDown(0))
            {
                ShootServerRPC();
            }

        }

    }
    [ServerRpc]
    void ShootServerRPC()
    {
        ShootClientRpc();
    }
    [ClientRpc]
    void ShootClientRpc()
    {
        var bullet = Instantiate(gunbullet, gun.position,
        Quaternion.identity);
        bullet.transform.position = gun.transform.position;

        //To do Bullet Hit Logic
    }
```

There is more than one player in a multiplayer game and since they will have the same movement script, you need to determine which component is the local player. This is because you will be playing the game locally and the other parts of the game are coming from the server.

To achieve this, the code checks whether you are a local payer and calls shootserverRPC, which will instruct the server to shoot a bullet using the RPC calls.

Summary

This chapter discussed common multiplayer gameplayer terms and dove into developing a multiplayer game. You learned how multiplayer games work and how the data is shared between the server and the players. To create this game, you used MLAPI of Unity, which is a mid-level networking library.

CHAPTER 7

LAN Networking

A Local Area Network (LAN) is a computer network that connects nearby devices, such as ones in a home, school, university, business, etc.

Most people with Internet connectivity use LAN networking in their homes. The ISP will provide only one connection, but you can use that same connection in multiple devices because of LAN networking. LAN networking setup includes a router, which routes your traffic internally and over the Internet. By using LAN with multiple devices and a router, you essentially have a mini-Internet at your disposal, as shown in Figure 7-1.

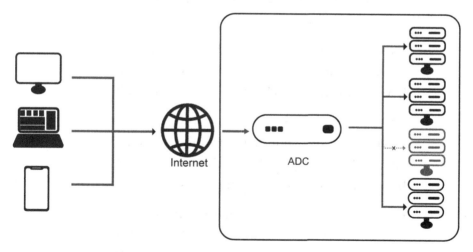

Figure 7-1. *A LAN with multiple devices and a router*

The original version of this chapter was revised. A correction to this chapter is available at https://doi.org/10.1007/978-1-4842-7358-6_9

© Sloan Kelly and Khagendra Kumar 2022, corrected publication 2022
S. Kelly and K. Kumar, *Unity Networking Fundamentals*,
https://doi.org/10.1007/978-1-4842-7358-6_7

Most people use the same network when hosting a LAN party to play a game. Whenever you start a server, it's actually starting the server on your machine. Since it's a local Internet and there is minimal restriction by the router, you can connect to any port of any computer or device from any computer or device internally. That means you can connect to a local LAN party and play your game.

Hamachi is a Virtual Private Networking (VPN) service. A VPN is protected from the global Internet via a router/modem (see Figure 7-2). The local Internet is often called an *intranet.*

In order to access LAN parties, players need to join from the same network or be available in same network. No one outside the local area network can find that server, as the router protects that server from external communications.

There are two ways to solve that problem:

- *Create an open server:* Create a server that's open to the world and open the required ports, to which anyone from anywhere can connect.

  This setup is not typically feasible because it exposes the networking devices and data and requires you to have a static IP, which is not available by default.

  This will additionally require you to set up a firewall service to protect your network from malicious activity. Your computer's default firewall might not be enough to protect you in these cases.

- *Create a VPN for your network and allow only trustworthy people to connect to it:* This way, you are not allowing everyone to join your network. VPN makes it possible to be part of a local network, so others have a direct tunnel to your LAN.

A VPN service provides privacy and anonymity to its users by masking their Internet to VPN networks. It then forwards the request to the desired client. Most VPN service providers doesn't keep logs in order to maintain the anonymity of their consumers.

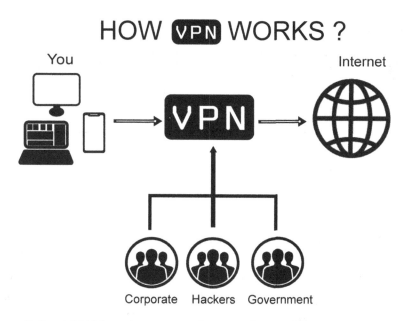

Figure 7-2. *A VPN protects your data and your identity*

How VPN Works

VPNs rely heavily on *virtual tunneling,* which is the ability to create a private tunnel to share data from one computer securely. VPN providers use a similar technique to create a tunnel from the client's computer to their network/location and then expose the data packet to the Internet. See Figure 7-3.

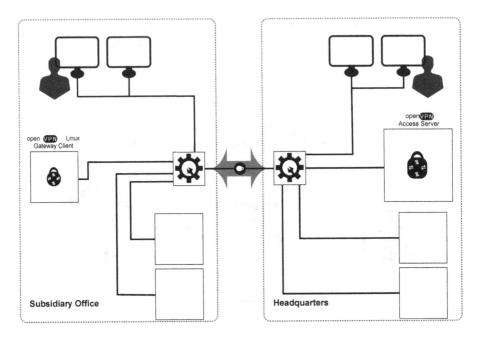

Figure 7-3. *VPNs use virtual tunneling*

Any attack on your system will be handled by the VPN. To securely transmit data from your computer to the VPN service, heavy encryption systems encrypt the data. In most cases, only the VPN can decrypt the data.

What Is Hamachi?

Hamachi is a very popular VPN service that's used to create local LAN parties across the Internet. The game that you created in this book cannot be played via the Internet, because a local server hosts the game and all the players must be connected to that same network.

Using Hamachi, however, you can bring other people into same VPN LAN party so they can play a local LAN party game over the Internet. A lot of gamers use these types of services to play with their friends.

Using Hamachi

Hamachi can be downloaded from its website; it's available for many platforms. Once you download and install Hamachi, it's very easy use. Follow these steps to set it up and use it:

1. Launch Hamachi.

2. Click the Power button to start Hamachi, as shown in Figure 7-4.

Figure 7-4. *Starting Hamachi*

3. Log in with your credentials if you're asked for them. After you do so, you will be logged in and the Hamachi service will start, as shown in Figure 7-5.

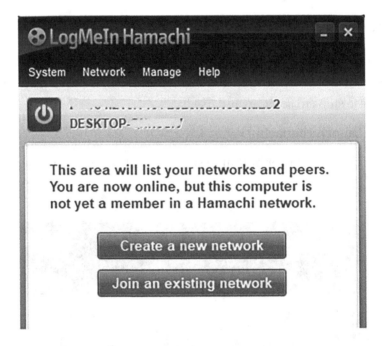

Figure 7-5. *Logging into Hamachi*

4. Note the IP address given to you next to the Start
    Service button.

5. If you are planning to host the game, click Create a
    New Network, as shown in Figure 7-6.

Figure 7-6. *Create a new network if you are hosting the game*

6. You will be prompted to enter the network ID and
    password (see Figure 7-7). This network ID and
    password must also be shared with friends who
    want to join the LAN party and play the game.

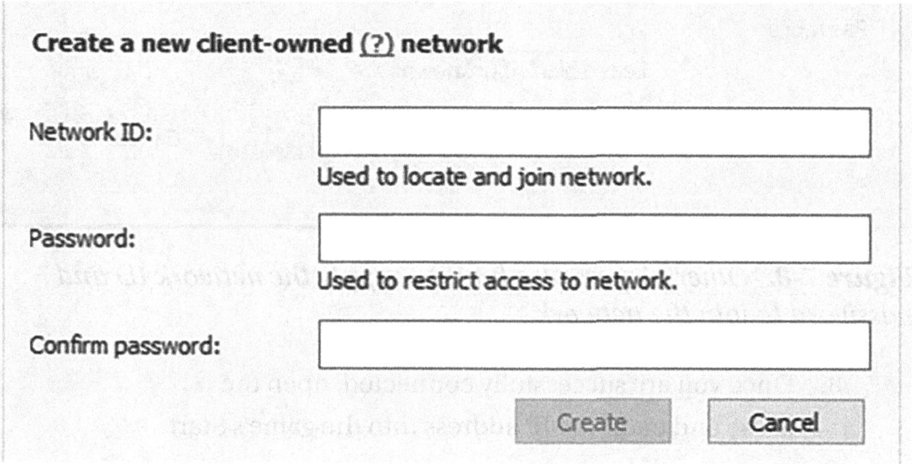

Create a new client-owned (?) network

Network ID:

Used to locate and join network.

Password:

Used to restrict access to network.

Confirm password:

Create   Cancel

Figure 7-7. Supply the network ID and password

7. Your friends should click the Join an Existing
    Network button to join your network. They will be
    prompted to enter the network ID and password as
    well, as shown in Figure 7-8.

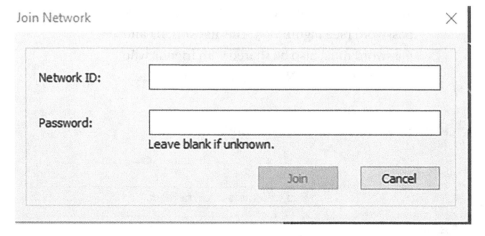

Figure 7-8. *Other players also have to supply the network ID and password to join the network*

> 8. Once you are successfully connected, open the
>   game and enter the IP address into the game's Start
>   screen to play the game.

LAN Party in Games

There are many ways that games leverage the LAN party concept. One very simple way is by creating a server on your computer. Then you scan for a local server, which usually scans for the ports that have been programmed by developers to be used for LAN party servers across the local network.

The newer and more popular way to create a LAN party is by creating a local WiFi network or by connecting all the devices to the same WiFi network.

Summary

This chapter talked about how LAN parties work. It discussed the major problems that arise when you try to connect to a LAN party from outside the network. The chapter also looked into how you can rectify these solutions using VPN.

You learned what a VPN is and how it solves these LAN party issues. You also learned how to create a VPN-based LAN party using Hamachi.

CHAPTER 8

Servers

Servers are like computers that sit at the other end of the network helping you do things. Servers are used for multiple purposes, including as webservers. They are used for data storage, loud storage, cloud computing, research, and for games as well.

Games use servers in different ways, which means the way the servers are developed is different as well (see Figure 8-1).

- Dedicated servers
- Listen servers
- Peer-to-peer networks

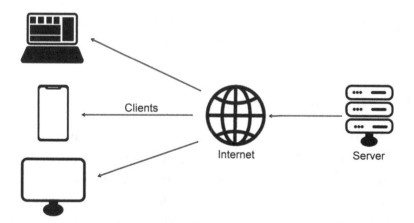

Figure 8-1. *Server and clients*

The original version of this chapter was revised. A correction to this chapter is available at https://doi.org/10.1007/978-1-4842-7358-6_9

© Sloan Kelly and Khagendra Kumar 2022, corrected publication 2022
S. Kelly and K. Kumar, *Unity Networking Fundamentals*,
https://doi.org/10.1007/978-1-4842-7358-6_8

What Is a Server?

A server is a computer that connects to different computers over the network to serve data over LANs (Local Area Networks) or WANs (Wide Area Networks).

You might have heard of different types of servers—email servers, web servers, file servers—these servers have similar hardware components whereas the software they run is unique.

Server software includes Apache, Nginx, and Microsoft IIS, which are most predominantly used for website hosting. Some SMTP servers used for email services include Exim, iMail, etc.

While any computer can be configured as a server, the major difference is the hardware design. Servers are designed to run around the clock without any hiccups. Many industries and big organizations don't use traditional computers for servers; they use especially designed cases for servers named as 1U, 2U, 3U and so on, the sizes of which vary upon their usage. These servers are typically mounted on hardware racks for storage.

Since these devices are capable of running with major interruptions and can be left alone, most of these servers are configured in a way that they can be controlled and managed remotely.

Dedicated Servers

Dedicated servers are exactly what they sound like. These servers are dedicated to one specific purpose, which can be for video streaming, web hosting, or for any other purpose. Most businesses prefer dedicated servers because of their immense power and flexibility. Servers are mostly used by websites over the Internet and most websites across the Internet are hosted on shared servers.

Shared servers are servers that host hundreds or thousands of websites. This makes renting server space a lot cheaper for owners who don't require a lot of storage and computational power. However, once they need to upgrade their plan, they can migrate to dedicated servers, which are usually known as VPSs (Virtual Private Servers).

With a VPS, you get a virtual computer, which you can configure according to your needs. A VPS is as flexible as dedicated servers to an extent. But this is still far from an actual dedicated server, which means you have access to the actual server. The major downsides to this kind of approach are cost and maintenance. As their devices are manufactured to run continuously in isolation, they also can be extremely loud and might require an ideal environment to operate at 100% capacity.

Who Should Get a Dedicated Server?

Consider these characteristics of dedicated servers:

- **Scalability**: Dedicated servers are very easy to scale up, which is beneficial for growth. For example, websites like Google and YouTube, which serve billions of users daily and are expected to grow, would burn a lot of money in renting servers.

- **Security**: Companies that deal with very sensitive data may not want to use dedicated servers. Keeping that data in a shared space is a big concern. If any of the websites or services hosted on that same shared space are compromised, the possibility of confidential data being leaked is significant.

  Any malicious web service could also rent the same server with bad intentions to compromise the service. They could infect the service with ransomware, virus-vulnerable code, or any other malicious activity.

- **Speed**: Shared services can lead to instability, depending on a load of the shared websites and this, in turn, can affect the performance of your services.

- **Control**: As discussed earlier, dedicated servers allow you to customize your services as needed, which means you have the power to offer non-traditional services, such as game builds, game streaming, etc.

Dedicated Servers in Gaming

Since the beginning of personal computers, private game servers/ dedicated game servers were always among the top choices for gaming platforms. This was preferrable to depending on a multiplayer service provider.

Creating your dedicated game server has a lot of benefits, including stability, customizability, and control. A lot of different multiplayer systems use dedicated game servers, including PUBG, ARK: Survival Evolved, Team Fortress 2, etc.

Most public game servers use the client-server model (discussed in Chapter 5) or peer-to-peer (P2P) hosting, both of which have their problems. Client servers are run by process owners, usually the publishers or manufacturer, and as a consequence they can manage individual connections. This model works in most cases, but it lags in terms of customizability options.

P2P (peer-to-peer networking) is another very popular modern multiplayer gaming service. Using P2P, one player can dynamically act as host or master, which can facilitate connections from other devices or players. This system is highly random, as anyone can be chosen as the host. If the host's network is poor, everyone will have a bad gaming experience.

Headless Server, AKA Listen Server

A *headless server* can be controlled over a network. These servers don't
have a keyboard, mouse, or any other peripherals. For example, servers
that are configured on rack mounts are typically headless servers, as
shown in Figure 8-2.

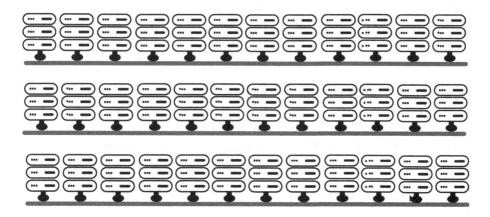

Figure 8-2. *Server racks in a datacenter*

A system without a head (a monitor) or without a local interface is also
headless. There need to be peripherals like a keyboard, mouse, screen,
or a local interface to control it. Headless systems lack graphical systems
to access and administer them, instead they are usually administered
remotely over a network, via SSH or VNC.

Why a Headless Server?

When we talk about servers, we mostly talk about datacenters and
very large server arrays that look like a sci-fi movie scene. In these
environments, computers are usually stacked on top of one another and

hundreds of racks of that type are placed together. These *server farms* or datacenters are controlled via networks and they rarely need human intervention for maintenance.

These systems are managed over the Internet so they don't need any peripherals except networking gear. Server hardware is getting smaller and more efficient, and these systems can run for years without any human intervention, provided the Internet and power are constantly provided. The popularity of headless servers is growing day by day.

Headless Servers in Games

In game-based dedicated servers, the server might act as a bot or be coordinating the actions of another player or playing by themselves as a bot. This is considered a dedicated gaming server and these types of games are usually multiplayer games. In this case, a headless server is mostly used for administrative purposes.

Many times, you'll want to play an online game where a server will be used mostly for administrative purposes. These servers do not have a graphical interface or have any human interaction from the server-side. For example, consider a game where every person has a task to complete and they are not competing with each other. The AI is running on a device, competing against a real human. Just for the sake of management and a sense of competitiveness, the server will be used to assign the level and AI parameters, which means the allocation and administrative jobs. In this case, it uses a headless server.

Peer-to-Peer Networks

As you might notice, we don't call these peer-to-peer servers because peer-to-peer communication is not considered server-based, per se.

When two or more devices connect to each other directly, without any entity in between, that's called a peer-to-peer network. The device trying to share the data is directly connected to the device waiting to receive the data.

Peer-to-Peer Networks in Games

This type of network is widely used with games that want to create a local group of players, such as with Counter Strike, Mini Militia, and many more. They can create a local server on which players can connect and then directly join the game. These kinds of network games are called peer-to-peer games. Because there is a local server, the delay and other networking issues will be minimized.

Benefits of a Peer-to-Peer Network

- **No central server**: Developers do not need to manage costly servers and handle all the networking issues.

- **No queue management**: Developers don't have to manage multiple game rooms and do matchmaking for players, as this is handled automatically by the players. The local network can support more than 10 people.

- **No downtime**: As most servers will be completely managed by the local players and there is very little dependency on the Internet, there isn't any downtime.

- **No loss of players**: In online games, developers have to deal with loss of players due to loss of network, rage quits, etc. These need to be handled and developers manage them by replacing the player with a bot. In this case, developers don't have to do that, as a local peer-to-peer setup reduces the chances of network dropout. Developers don't need to use bots either.

Load Balancers

As the name suggests, the basic functionality of a load balancer is to help the datacenter balance the load between the servers. It can also be seen as a tool to distribute the workload request from the client to different servers in order to optimize the delivery time and effective utilization of servers.

A load balancer can be a physical device or a virtual device running along the server to process incoming requests and control the assigning of requests to different servers. This is also known as Application Delivery Controllers (ADCs) and this type of system is designed to improve the performance and security of systems (see Figure 8-3). They predominantly use scheduling algorithms like Round-Robin, SJFS, and many more to effectively manage loads.

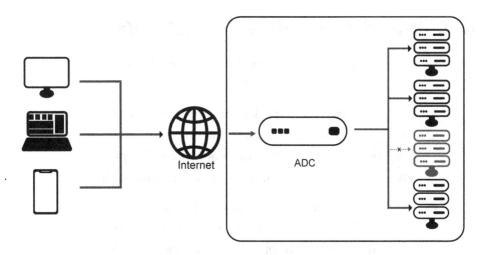

Figure 8-3. *Load balancing ADC*

Load balancers are a crucial part of the modern Internet infrastructure, a load balancing-capable ADC will help the IT department ensure secure scalability by ensuring 100% availability of services. Their advanced functionality of traffic management can help businesses and consumers efficiently serve customer requests while maintaining efficient usage of hardware resources. An ADC might offer additional services to enhance security and flexibility, such as firewall protection, data encryption, and DDOS protection.

A load balancer can be of two types (see Figure 8-4):

- Hardware based

- Software based

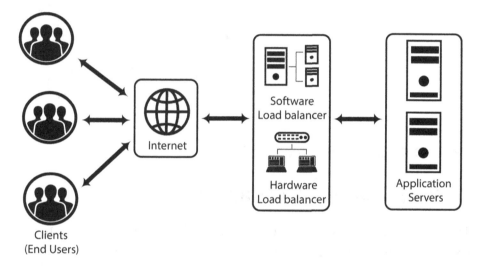

Figure 8-4. *Load balancer types*

Hardware-Based Load Balancers

Hardware-based load balancers are capable of securely managing and processing hundreds of gigabits of traffic from multiple sources. They also have built-in virtualization capabilities that allow them to be configured as an army of load balancers for some specific use cases. This kind of flexibility provides a multi-tenant architecture with full isolation, along with other benefits. See Figure 8-5.

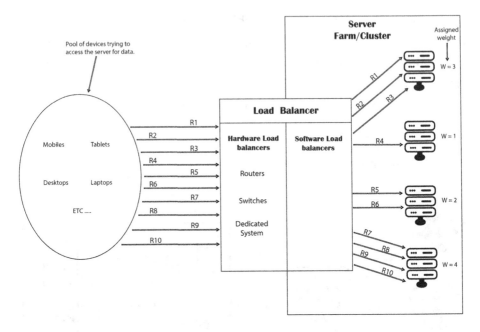

Figure 8-5. *Load balancing switching*

Software-Based Load Balancers

The job of load balancers is to manage the load or incoming traffic, and software-based load balancers can be installed on any hypervisor to ensure the functionality of load balancers. They can run on the same server using a hypervisor or they can be run inside containers of Linux subsystems to reduce the load on an existing server. This can save a lot of space and hardware expense.

Summary

The chapter started with a discussion of servers and how they work. You learned about server segregation based on game systems, like dedicated, headless, and P2P servers, and you also learned about how these servers are used in games.

Correction to: Unity Networking Fundamentals

Sloan Kelly and Khagendra Kumar

Correction to:

Chapters 5, 7 & 8 in: **Sloan Kelly and Khagendra Kumar,** *Unity Networking Fundamentals:* **Creating Multiplayer Games with Unity**

https://doi.org/10.1007/978-1-4842-7358-6

The original version of the chapters 5, 7 & 8 images was inadvertently published with the incorrect artworks for these chapters. The correct figures with text labels are given below:

The updated online version of these chapters can be found at
https://doi.org/10.1007/978-1-4842-7358-6_5
https://doi.org/10.1007/978-1-4842-7358-6_7
https://doi.org/10.1007/978-1-4842-7358-6_8

© Sloan Kelly and Khagendra Kumar 2022
S. Kelly and K. Kumar, *Unity Networking Fundamentals,*
https://doi.org/10.1007/978-1-4842-7358-6_9

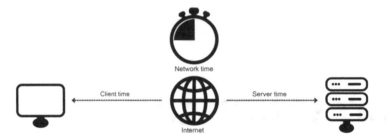

Figure 5-1. *Latency representation*

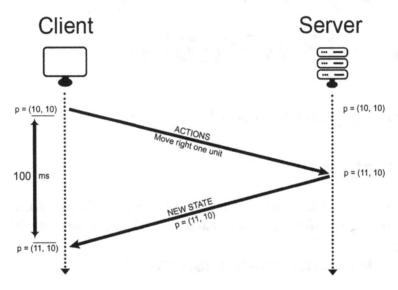

Figure 5-3. *Representation of network delay*

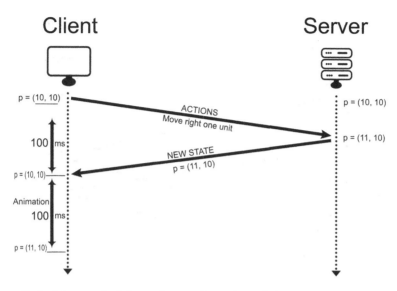

Figure 5-4. *Network delay plus animation delay*

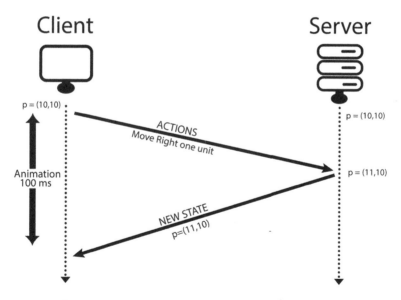

Figure 5-5. *Playing animation during network delay*

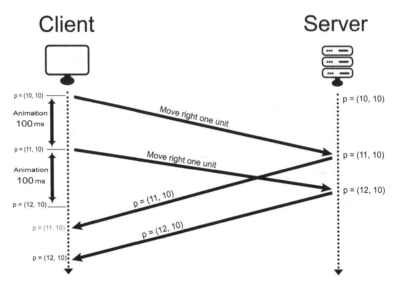

Figure 5-6. *Predictive state mismatch with an authoritative server*

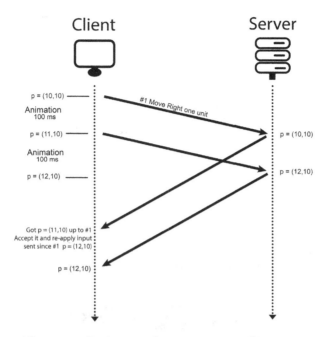

Figure 5-7. *Client prediction and server reconciliation*

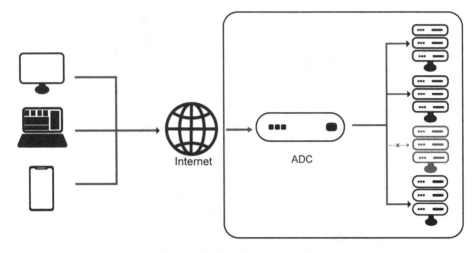

Figure 7-1. *A LAN with multiple devices and a router*

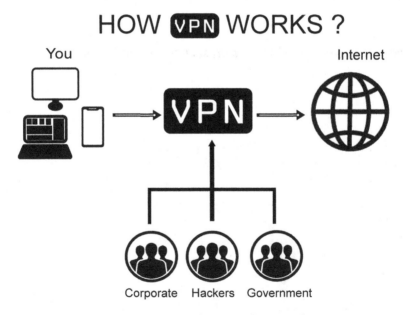

Figure 7-2. *A VPN protects your data and your identity*

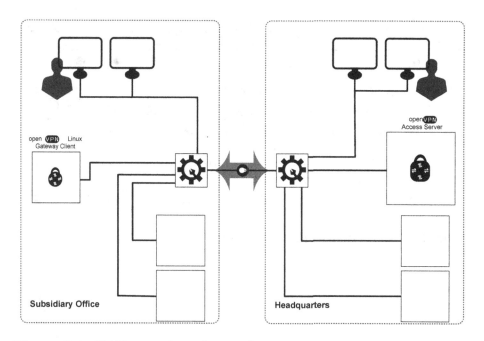

Figure 7-3. *VPNs use virtual tunneling*

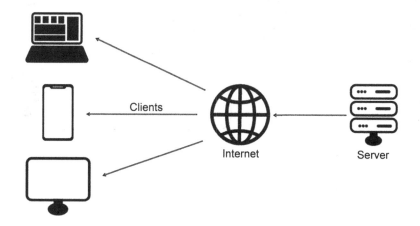

Figure 8-1. *Server and clients*

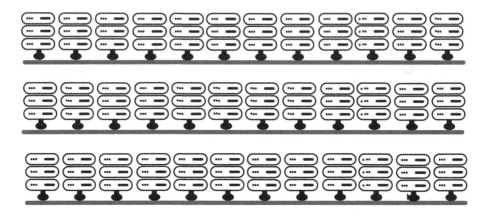

Figure 8-2. *Server racks in a datacenter*

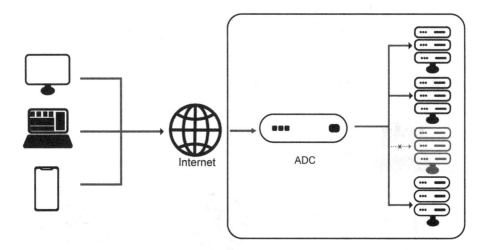

Figure 8-3. *Load balancing ADC*

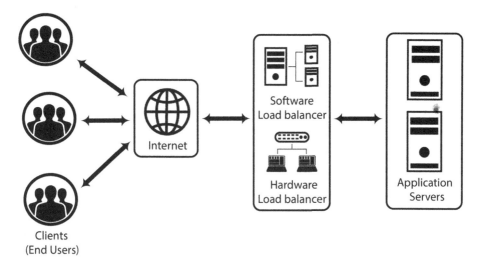

Figure 8-4. *Load balancer types*

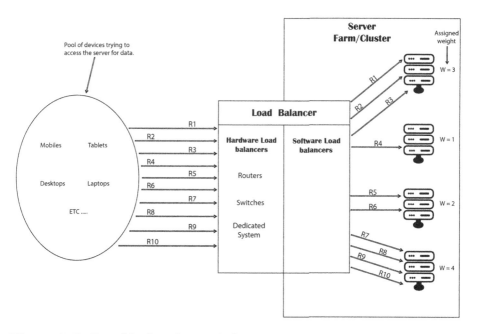

Figure 8-5. *Load balancing switching*

Index

© Sloan Kelly and Khagendra Kumar 2022
S. Kelly and K. Kumar, *Unity Networking Fundamentals*,
https://doi.org/10.1007/978-1-4842-7358-6

T

Printed in the United States
by Baker & Taylor Publisher Services